OXFORD

WALKS BESIDE THE RIVER CHERWELL

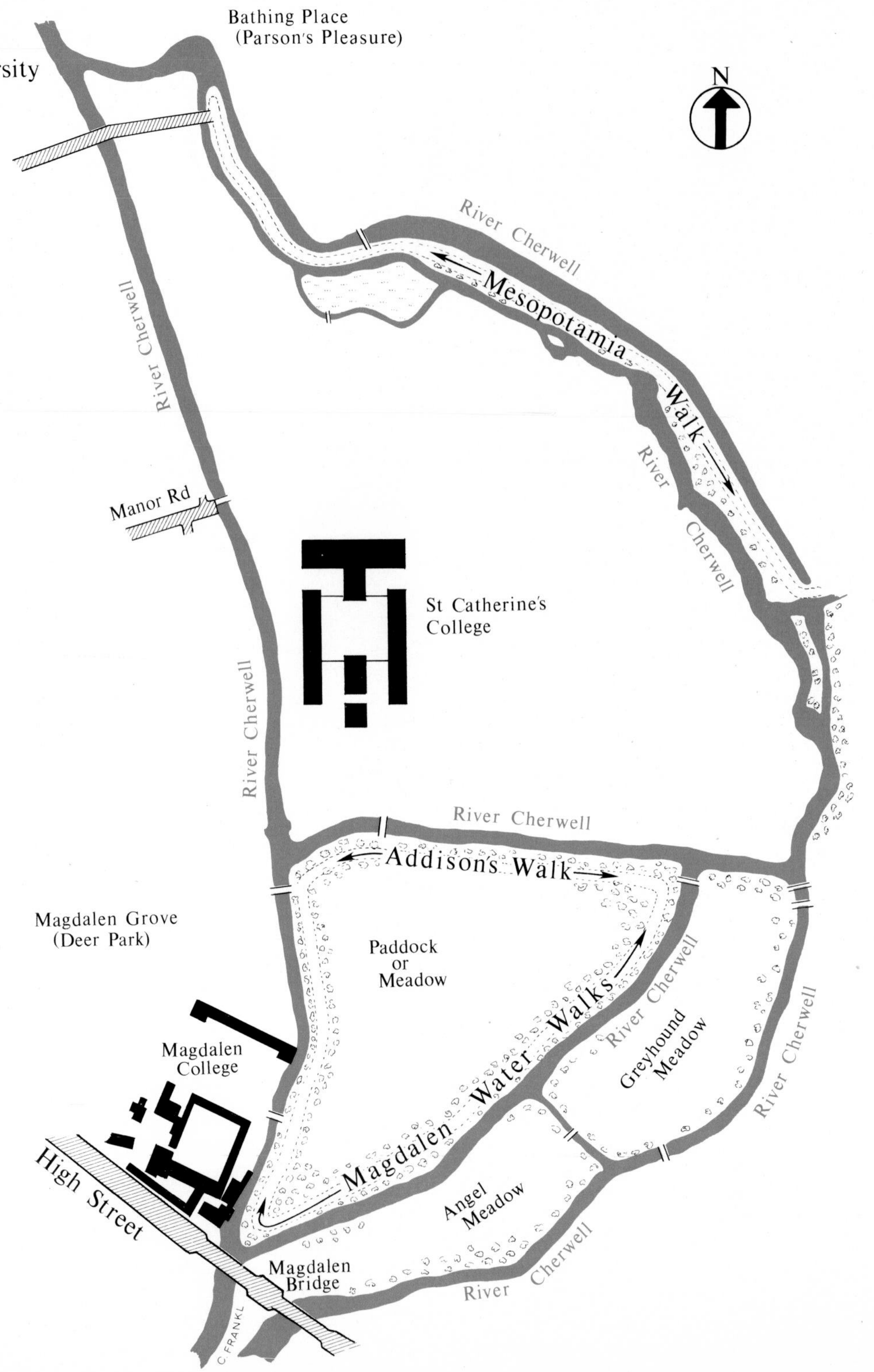

Bathing Place
(Parson's Pleasure)

To University Parks

N

River Cherwell

River Cherwell

Mesopotamia Walk

River Cherwell

Manor Rd

St Catherine's College

River Cherwell

River Cherwell

Addisons Walk

Magdalen Grove
(Deer Park)

Paddock or Meadow

River Cherwell

Magdalen Water Walks

Greyhound Meadow

River Cherwell

River Cherwell

Magdalen College

Angel Meadow

High Street

Magdalen Bridge

River Cherwell

River

C. FRANKL

THE HISTORIC CENTRE

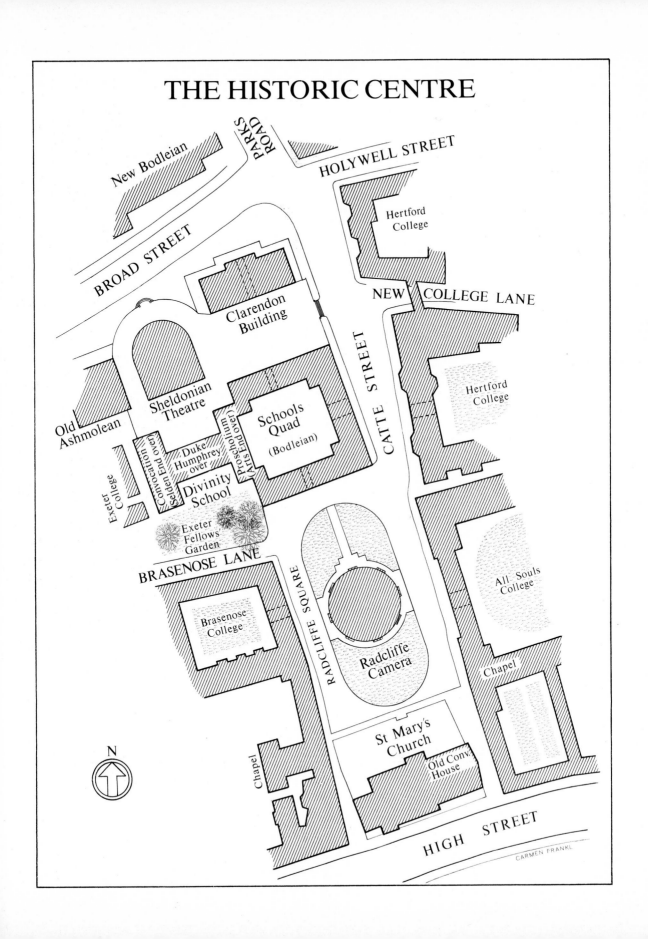

New Bodleian

PARKS ROAD

HOLYWELL STREET

Hertford College

BROAD STREET

Clarendon Building

NEW COLLEGE LANE

Sheldonian Theatre

Old Ashmolean

CATTE STREET

Hertford College

Schools Quad (Bodleian)

Exeter College

Convocation over (Selden End over)

Duke Humphrey over

Proscholium (Arts End over)

Divinity School

Exeter Fellows' Garden

BRASENOSE LANE

All Souls College

RADCLIFFE SQUARE

Brasenose College

Radcliffe Camera

Chapel

Chapel

St Mary's Church

Old Conv. House

N

HIGH STREET

CARMEN FRANKL

OXFORD

Text by
MICHAEL HALL

With photographs by
ERNEST FRANKL

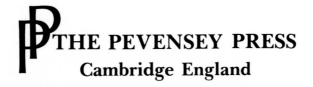

THE PEVENSEY PRESS
Cambridge England

Front cover All Souls College towers (1714-20), designed by Hawksmoor, seen from St Mary's Church. In the foreground is the college chapel; behind the towers is New College Chapel

◄ *Frontispiece* Looking through the gateway in the screen of All Souls College North Quad towards the Radcliffe Camera (1737-49). The architect of North Quad, Hawksmoor, also designed this wrought-iron gate (1734), for a fee of one guinea. Until 1863 the grilles around the base of the Camera were unglazed

Back cover Worcester College: a glimpse of the gardens through an archway in the south range of the quad

Published by The Pevensey Press
6 De Freville Avenue, Cambridge CB4 1HR, UK

Photographs: Ernest Frankl, except 15: from Bodleian Library Film Strip 194A; 20: Ashmolean Museum, Oxford; 23: Nicholas Servian FIIP, Woodmansterne Ltd; 49: Howard C. Moore, Woodmansterne Ltd; 78: Ruth Smith; 80: Charlotte Hall

Maps: Carmen Frankl

The assistance of Dr Helen Cooper, Miss Ann Johnston, Mr Eric van Tassel and Mr William Wood is gratefully acknowledged

Edited by Ruth Smith

Designed by Tim McPhee
Design and production in association with Book Production Consultants, Cambridge

First published 1981
Second edition 1983

ISBN 0 907115 12 8

Typesetting in Baskerville by Westholme Graphics Ltd

Printed in Hong Kong

Contents

1 TOWN AND GOWN   1

2 UNIVERSITY BUILDINGS   17

3 THE COLLEGES   31

    All Souls College   31
    Balliol College   32
    Brasenose College   34
    Christ Church   36
    Corpus Christi College   42
    Exeter College   44
    Hertford College   44
    Jesus College   45
    Lincoln College   48
    Magdalen College   50
    Merton College   56
    New College   59
    Oriel College   65
    Pembroke College   67
    The Queen's College   68
    St Edmund Hall   71
    St John's College   72
    Trinity College   75
    University College   78
    Wadham College   80
    Worcester College   82
    19th- and 20th-century colleges   84

4 LIFE IN THE MODERN UNIVERSITY   93

Maps

    Front: Walks beside the River Cherwell
             The Historic Centre
    Back: North Oxford
            South Oxford

1 Town and Gown

According to legend, at the beginning of the 8th century Frideswide, a princess who had vowed to become a nun, fled to Oxford to escape an unwanted suitor. Her pursuer was struck blind as he entered the town; her prayers restored his sight, and in gratitude he gave up the chase. Frideswide stayed in Oxford and founded a priory where she was eventually buried, and later she was canonised. Her story represents the earliest tradition of a settlement at what is now Oxford, and archaeological evidence suggests that there may indeed have been a church on the site of St Frideswide's Priory (where Christ Church is now) in the 8th century. Oxford may have originated as a settlement outside the priory gates. The medieval chroniclers gave it a more glamorous history: Geoffrey of Monmouth, who wrote his *History of the Kings of Britain* here, numbered it amongst the cities of King Arthur's realm. In fact the first attested reference to Oxford is as late as 912, when the *Anglo-Saxon Chronicle* records that Edward the Elder (a son of King Alfred) took control of the town and the surrounding area, which occupied an important strategic position between his territory in Wessex and country held by the Danes.

The town owes its name to its location on a major crossing-point of the Thames. The exact whereabouts of the original ford have been much debated: probably it was near the present Magdalen Bridge. Being at the centre of southern England, Oxford was on important lines of communication, linked by road and the River Thames to London and to the Midlands by the Cherwell, a navigable tributary of the Thames. From the first it was a market town, for it lay on two major trade routes, from the Midlands to Southampton and from London to Gloucester and the Welsh border.

1 St Michael's Church, Cornmarket Street: the late Saxon tower (c1000-50), Oxford's oldest building, stands beside the site of the North Gate (demolished 1771); it was important to Oxford's defences, serving as a look-out and stronghold. The rest of the church is mostly 13th century. The timber-framed shop on the right is probably 15th century

A reminder of Saxon Oxford survives in the city's regular street plan, probably first laid out by Edward the Elder. The ancient centre is oblong, and was enclosed by a wall with four gates. Roads ran between the north and south gates (roughly on the line of Cornmarket and St Aldate's Streets) and between the east and west gates (on the line of the High and Queen Streets). Their intersection, at the city's centre, is called Carfax (from the French *quatre voies*, four ways). Oxford's only remaining Saxon building, the tower of the Church of St Michael at the North Gate (1), was built c1000-50.

By 1066 Oxford had expanded far beyond the town walls, and with about 1000 houses and 11 churches was the sixth largest town in England. It was often at the centre of political life: here Harold Harefoot was elected king (1036) and Edmund Ironside died mysteriously (1016), and Edward the Confessor was born nearby in 1005. The Normans established control over Oxford with the

1

◄**2** *The High Street (from St Mary's), usually called 'The High' (similarly Broad Street is called 'The Broad'). Foreground, All Souls College gate-tower; left, the Queen's College and the gables of St Edmund Hall's new building; right, University College, with the spire of the 19th-century Examination Schools behind, Magdalen College beyond and Headington in the distance*

▼**3** *One of the last surviving sections of the 13th-century city wall, complete with bastions and rampart walk, in New College garden*

building of the Castle (1071), erected by Robert d'Oilly as a royal residence and centre of county administration. During the 12th-century civil war Queen Matilda made the Castle her headquarters and was besieged in it for three months (she made her escape across the frozen river, camouflaged in a white sheet); and here King Stephen met the future Henry II and agreed to end the war. The Castle was rebuilt in the Middle Ages, but was not used for military purposes after 1322, until it was garrisoned in turn by both Royalist and Parliamentary troops in the 17th century. Today all that remains of it is the Norman mound and the tower of the Church of St George-in-the-Castle (1074), originally part of the defences.

The fortunes of the town declined at the end of the 11th century, but the wool and cloth trades brought it temporary prosperity. Religious foundations were established: St Frideswide's Priory, refounded in 1122, was joined by Osney Abbey (1129, the third largest in the country) and Godstow Priory (1133). Most of the townspeople still lived within the city walls, which had been extended and rebuilt in the early 11th century (**3**). The width of some of the streets, notably St Giles and Broad Streets, is a survival of the markets held in them during the Middle Ages. The medieval name of Broad Street, Horsemongers' Lane, shows that a regular horse fair was probably held there.

The town's decline coincided with the establishment and growth of the University, which dominated Oxford's history for the next 700 years. The University was long believed to have been founded by King Alfred – a tradition accepted well into the 19th century, when it was proposed to erect a statue of the king in Broad Street. In fact, the University was never founded: it gradually

evolved. Scholars were teaching in Oxford before 1117, perhaps as early as the 1090s; the establishment of religious houses and the building of a royal palace at nearby Woodstock attracted more, and they were added to by migrations from the scholarly communities of Paris and Northampton. Oxford had several advantages – it was central, relatively rich and, unlike the political centres of London and Winchester, quiet. It was not, before 1542, the seat of a bishopric, and so the academic community was free from interference by local prelates. The first reference to a University Chancellor, indicating an organised university, occurs in 1214, but the office was probably in existence before then.

Relations between town and gown were bad to begin with and rapidly worsened. The influx of scholars (membership of the medieval University varied between 1500 and 3000) was a considerable strain on the self-supporting community, which suddenly had to provide for large numbers of people who were, in economic terms, merely consumers and produced nothing themselves. The townspeople naturally made the best of the situation by charging high prices and rents. The University naturally attempted to interfere with the fixing of prices to protect its members; the town resented both this and the University's many legal privileges. A serious riot occurred in 1209, when a student killed a local woman and some townspeople lynched two innocent scholars in retaliation. The University disbanded and fled, some scholars going to Cambridge, to create or enlarge another university there. A papal ordinance (1214) imposed fines and penances on the town and instituted a system of rent control, very much in the University's favour. This was the first of many violent conflicts with the same outcome: the University, backed by royal and ecclesi-

astical approval, was strengthened at the expense of the town. The academic population returned and was soon reinforced by the friars. The Dominicans began teaching in Oxford in 1221 and the Franciscans in 1224, and their presence led to greater emphasis on theology in the University's curriculum. By now Oxford had a European reputation for its teaching of mathematics and natural sciences.

The poor discipline exercised by the University over its students also caused contention with the town. This was something the University tried hard to improve, by establishing control over student accommodation. Before colleges existed students could rent a whole house for themselves (which rarely happened, as most students were poor), or take only a room in an inn or private house, or live in a hall (hostel). The halls were houses leased from a local landlord, usually by a Master of Arts in the University who took responsibility for the students living there and gave them some tuition. In about 1410 the University made residence in halls compulsory for all its students, so that none would be beyond its jurisdiction.

The colleges, on the other hand, were designed to cater for graduate students. Medieval university education was very protracted; for instance, a student was not eligible for a doctorate in theology until 16 years after he had matriculated (entered the University). Few students could afford to stay at the University long enough to take a degree in the higher faculties of law, theology or medicine, but there was a need for well-educated lawyers, clerics and doctors. This was the reason for the founding of the first colleges, which were endowed, unlike the halls, and so could house and maintain scholars unable to support themselves.

▼ **6** *Reflections in the Cherwell. Oxford stands on two rivers, the Thames and its tributary the Cherwell. The broader Thames (to the south and west of the city), once important for trade, is used for boat races; the winding Cherwell with its many streams flowing through meadows to the east of Oxford (see **9, 42** and front map) is ideal for expeditions in a punt. The Thames is known in Oxford as the Isis, perhaps from 'Thamesis', the river's Latin name*

► **7** *Carfax Tower: the clock, and the quarterjacks which strike the quarter-hours. The original jacks, replaced in 1898, can be seen in the City Museum in St Aldate's. The 14th-century tower belonged to the City Church of St Martin (demolished 1896) and bears the city's motto. During the Middle Ages it served as a fortress and vantage-point in the frequent battles between town and gown. The University complained to Edward III that townspeople flung stones and shot arrows from the tower; the king ordered that the topmost section be removed. One of the chimes for Carfax clock was composed by John Stainer*

FORTIS EST VERITAS

9 *Magdalen meadows from the college's water walks: such rural tranquillity, only a few hundred yards from the noisy traffic of the High Street, is one of Oxford's greatest delights*

◄8 *The Chequers Inn, off the High Street (15th-17th century), one of the several ancient inns remaining in the city centre. Others include the Mitre, the Turf Tavern and the Golden Cross*

Their founders were frequently very rich men, and their large and splendid buildings changed the appearance of Oxford as the impoverished University and humble halls had not. The first college was Merton, founded in 1264. University College was in existence by *c*1280 and Balliol followed in 1282. Until the 16th century the colleges were mainly small and select communities of postgraduates – as All Souls has remained to this day – but from 1379, following the pattern set by William of Wykeham's New College, they began to accommodate undergraduates as well.

In 1355 there was a crisis in the relations between town and gown. On 10 February, St Scholastica's Day, two scholars, Walter Spryngheuse and Roger de Chesterfield, visited the Swindlestock Tavern at Carfax (the site is marked by a plaque); during a quarrel, possibly about the quality of the drink, one of them flung a quart pot of wine in the innkeeper's face. A brawl developed, the innkeeper's friends rang the bells of the City Church of St Martin to summon assistance, and the scholars were rallied by the bells of the University Church, St Mary's. To avoid large-scale rioting the town's bailiffs demanded that the Chancellor arrest the scholars who began the fight; when he refused they set off for Woodstock, to lay their grievances before the king, and in the ensuing riot several scholars were killed and the rest fled to the king for protection. Nevertheless, the final outcome of this sordid event was that the University assumed a total ascendancy over the town which it enjoyed until the 19th century. The Mayor was sent to prison. The Chancellor was given new powers to control the markets and assess rents. The townspeople had to pay a substantial fine to the University and the Mayor and bailiffs were forced to attend an annual Mass for the souls of the scholars slain in the riot – a penance not finally abolished until 1825.

In 1344 Oxford was – on the basis of taxable wealth – the eighth richest provincial town in England; by 1523 it was the twenty-ninth. It no longer had political importance except as the seat of the University. Its position as the head of navigation on the Thames was taken over by Henley. The fall in population caused by the decline of the wool and wine trades and the devastation of the plague enabled the University and colleges to acquire much of central Oxford, the commercial centre contracting to a small area around Carfax. The town's decay was partly offset by the University's expanding role as an employer. Slowly the economic base of Oxford changed from manufacture and commerce to service trades, such as victualling and bookbinding, dependent on the University.

In the late 14th and early 15th centuries Oxford became notorious for housing the Lollards, the heretical followers of Wyclif, who had taught in the University (see under Balliol, Lincoln and Queen's Colleges). This troubled time was followed by peaceful changes as a revived interest in classical learning began to reach Oxford from Italy, stimulated by gifts of manuscripts from Henry V's brother Duke Humphrey, and by the presence of such scholars as Erasmus, John Colet and Sir Thomas More. In 1478 the first Oxford book was printed. In the early 16th century Oxford was visited by Protestants from Cambridge, but despite their influence it remained the more orthodox and traditional of the two universities. This brought it favour under the Catholic Queen Mary Tudor, when Protestant scholars were forced to flee the country. Archbishop Cranmer and Bishops Ridley and Latimer, the chief propagators of the new religion – all educated at Cambridge – were imprisoned in Oxford, and Cranmer was tried in St Mary's (1555), where the marks left by the erection of his dock can still be seen. All three bishops were burnt at the stake outside Balliol in Broad Street – an iron cross in the road marks the spot; Balliol's doors (still in existence) were singed by the fire.

During Elizabeth's reign it became fashionable for the gentry and aristocracy to send their sons to Oxford as the preliminary to a career in politics and the civil service. Learning flourished; although theology was still pre-eminent, geography, mathematics, archaeology and astrology were all studied with enthusiasm. Oxford was closely involved in the Civil War of the following century. On 29 October 1642, six days after his victory at Edgehill, Charles I made a state entry into the city, and for the next three and a half years Oxford was the Royalist capital. The University loyally supported the king: its Chancellor, Archbishop Laud, was one of his most devoted adherents. But the town, like most merchant communities, favoured the Parliamentarian cause and resented having to finance Royalist fortifications; however, it was never openly disloyal. Magdalen and New Colleges were turned into arsenals, provisions were stored in Brasenose and uniforms were made in the Astronomy School. The king held court at Christ Church and the queen at Merton; soldiers were billeted through the city. Teaching largely ceased, and most of the colleges gave their gold and silver plate to the king to be melted down. Oxford was twice besieged (1644, 1646), the second time successfully. In April the king fled and two months later the town surrendered to Parliamentarian forces.

The many scientists working in Oxford at the time of the Restoration in-

► **10** *The covered market, between the High Street and Cornmarket Street, designed by John Gwynn and opened in 1774 to house Oxford's market stalls, which had previously occupied the surrounding streets. The market's cafés, famous for their breakfasts, are popular with students and stallholders alike*

cluded Christopher Wren (then the Savilian Professor of Astronomy), Robert Hooke, and Robert Boyle who, in his house opposite All Souls, constructed the first practical air-pump and developed Boyle's Law of the expansion of gases. The 18th century, in contrast, is traditionally regarded as a time of stagnation. The historian Gibbon (at Magdalen 1752-3) recorded in his autobiography that 'the fellows of my time were decent, easy men . . . their days were filled by . . . the chapel and the hall, the coffee-house and the common-room, till they retired, weary and well satisfied, to a long slumber. From the toil of reading or thinking or writing they had absolved their conscience.' There was, however, some isolated intellectual activity: for instance, the foundations of Anglo-Saxon studies were laid at Oxford during this period. The indifference of the authorities in matters of religious observance stimulated John and Charles Wesley to initiate what became one of the world's great Christian movements, Methodism (see under Lincoln College). The 18th century was also the most glorious period of Oxford architecture, and saw the erection of the Radcliffe Camera (**22**), the Clarendon Building (**17**) and later the Observatory (**75**). The Queen's College was completely rebuilt and almost every other college, notably Christ Church, All Souls and Worcester, acquired new and beautiful extensions. In addition the University was presented with several ambitious schemes for remodelling the centre of Oxford; Hawksmoor proposed two great forums, one for the University on Radcliffe Square and one for the town on Carfax, and the replacing of St Mary's with a University temple in the classical style to the east of the Bodleian. Meanwhile the town made less drastic improvements, widening and paving streets and rebuilding Magdalen Bridge and the Town Hall. The Radcliffe Infirmary on the Woodstock Road (1759-70) was financed by the trustees of Dr John Radcliffe's will (it now has additional large new premises at Headington, begun in 1968). The market was moved off the streets into a covered enclosure opened in 1774 (**10**). The Oxford Canal was completed in 1790 and for ten halcyon years the city was at the midpoint of the shortest route by water between London and the Midlands. But trade on this route was abruptly cut by the opening of the Grand Junction Canal in 1800; although it recovered well, it declined in the 20th century and the Oxford Canal was closed to commercial traffic in 1955.

The University at last began to reform itself in the 19th century. The modern examination system was instigated in 1801, but at first only a minority of undergraduates took the exams. In 1850 a Royal Commission criticised Oxford for its failure to encourage learning or research. This was a reflection on the bitter theological controversy which had dominated Oxford life for 20 years, to the virtual exclusion of educational reform. Like Wesley in the previous century, the Tractarians (named for the tracts they wrote) wished to rid Oxford of its worldliness and persuade the colleges to inculcate students with spiritual and moral awareness. Their leaders, Keble, Pusey, Newman and Froude, were men of compelling personality who soon had a considerable undergraduate following. The fear that their theology was pro-Catholic made them unpopular with the orthodox senior members of the University, and the Martyrs' Memorial (1841-3; **11**), in memory of the Protestant Martyrs, was in part an anti-Catholic gesture inspired by the opponents of the Oxford Movement – as Tractarianism had come to be known. When in 1845 Newman was received into the Catholic Church there was a national sensation, and the Oxford Movement collapsed, in Oxford at least. Theological controversy ceased to dominate

University affairs; new subjects were introduced, buildings were erected for scientific teaching and research and undergraduate numbers rose dramatically. Oxford's influence in public life expanded, largely following the energetic reforms introduced by Jowett, the master of Balliol who ruthlessly raised educational standards in his college. Having for long been chiefly devoted to preparing men for the Church, Oxford turned into a forcing-house for the professions – medicine, law, politics, teaching and the civil service – and educated the men who ran the Empire. Organised games were encouraged for the first time, and the Oxford of popular mythology, a place of punts and champagne, boaters and *Charley's Aunt*, took shape. The seal was set on the secularisation of Oxford education by the abolition (1871) of the religious test, the declaration of faith in the 39 Articles, which students formerly had to take before receiving degrees.

The town grew considerably in the 19th century, stimulated by the arrival of the railway in 1843. The major single employer was the University Press; its move to Walton Street (west Oxford) in 1830 encouraged the speculative building of several streets of artisans' houses in the area known as Jericho (from the name of a local street and not, as was popularly supposed, because the houses were so flimsy that they would fall down at a trumpet blast). Subsequently north Oxford was developed as a pleasant suburb of villas in the Venetian Gothic style popularised by Ruskin, Slade Professor of Fine Art in the University. They were initially taken by wealthy tradesmen and after 1877, when the University lifted its age-old restrictions on marriage, by dons with

12, 13 *Victorian domestic architecture in Oxford; below, one of the Regency-style crescents in the Park Town estate, laid out 1853-5 – the earliest residential development in North Oxford – contrasts with (right) one of the many Gothic villas erected in this area after 1860*

families (**13**). In 1899 Oxford was elevated to county borough status and the Council took on the full range of local governmental powers. The building of a pompous Town Hall in St Aldate's in 1893-7 (designed by H. T. Hare) followed a tour by Councillors of major industrial towns of the Midlands and the north to seek models for monuments appropriate to Oxford's new status. The city soon emulated these towns more fully, by the growth of its own industry in the 20th century.

In 1901 William Morris opened a bicycle repair shop at 48 High Street; in 1902 he began to make motorcycles at a garage at the corner of Longwall and Holywell Streets; and in 1913 he produced his first car, the Morris Oxford. This was so successful that he established a factory at Cowley, east of the city, to assemble cars from standard parts made elsewhere. He was helped by Oxford's central position and large supply of cheap labour, and by 1925 he was making 41% of all cars produced in the United Kingdom. His success attracted related industries to Oxford and brought the city such wealth that by 1936 it was (with Coventry and Luton) one of the most prosperous towns in England. The Morris works at Cowley are still Oxford's largest employer, although recently there has been much effort to diversify, the dependence of the city on a single industry proving no healthier than its dependence on the University in past centuries. Morris, later Lord Nuffield, founded a graduate college and was in other ways a great benefactor to the University, particularly its medical department, but locally he is chiefly celebrated for restoring the fortunes of the city after it had lived for 700 years in the shadow of one of the world's greatest universities.

2 University Buildings

The earliest focus of University activities was the **Church of St Mary the Virgin** (**14**, **50**): here the archives were housed, ceremonies took place and Congregation (the governing body) convened. The oldest part of the present building is the late-13th-century tower; the richly ornamented spire was added 1315-25. To the north of the chancel is Congregation House (early 14th century), used for its original purpose until 1488. The University received gifts of books from the beginning of the 13th century, and in 1320 Bishop Cobham of Worcester financed the building of a library room over the Congregation House – the oldest surviving library building in England. The rest of the church is mainly late 15th century.

The first schools (faculty) buildings, where lectures were given, were simply hired rooms nearby. As theology was the most important subject in the medieval curriculum, the first purpose-built lecture room was the **Divinity School**, begun in 1420 but not completed for 70 years – for the University's architectural ambitions were beyond its means. The effects of economy and changing taste are clearly visible below the easternmost windows, where some of the mouldings terminate abruptly, the master mason having been ordered (in 1440) to dispense with the elaborate ornament originally planned. The glory of the Divinity School is the vault, completed in 1483. It was probably designed by William Orchard, whose initials are on one of the bosses. He devised the pendants that appear to support the complex lierne vaulting, which thus seems magically to hang suspended over the heavy transverse arches. This is the precursor of the larger vaults at St George's Chapel, Windsor, and Henry VII's Chapel, Westminster Abbey; it incorporates 455 bosses, carved into the coats of arms and monograms of those who financed the building, religious subjects, and animal and other motifs.

The Divinity School dates from the period when humanist learning was being introduced into Oxford, principally by Duke Humphrey of Gloucester, brother of Henry V. This eminent patron of Italian scholars in England helped to finance the Divinity School and presented the University with a collection of texts and commentaries that revealed a new range of classical learning to Oxford scholars. To house this library a room was constructed over the Divinity School. Now a reading room of the Bodleian Library, it is still referred to as 'Duke Humphrey'.

The duke's great collection was dispersed in the 16th century, but Thomas Bodley, diplomat and fellow of Merton, assembled 2000 books to form the basis of a new library, opened in 1602. The **Bodleian Library**, one of the greatest

◄**14** *St Mary's Church: the South Porch (1637), designed by Nicholas Stone. Despite the fashionable baroque exterior, inside the porch there is a Gothic fan vault. Stone possibly copied the twisting columns from Raphael's tapestry cartoon 'The Healing of the Lame Man in the Temple' in the set purchased by Charles I and now in the Victoria and Albert Museum, London. The porch was paid for by Dr Owen, chaplain to Archbishop Laud, the University's Chancellor; the inclusion of a statue of the Virgin outraged Puritan opinion and formed one of the charges against Laud at his trial. During the Civil War it was damaged by the shots of a disapproving Parliamentarian soldier*

libraries in the world, is now one of the five copyright libraries of the United Kingdom, empowered by the 1911 Copyright Act to demand one copy of every book published in this country – a privilege which can be traced back to the agreement Bodley made with the Stationers' Company in London, in 1610, that a copy of every book entered at Stationers' Hall should go to his library. Today the Bodleian contains some 4,000,000 books (excluding periodicals), and its holding of manuscripts and early printed books is second in this country only to that of the British Library.

At the east end of the Divinity School is the Proscholium or vestibule, now the main entrance to the Bodleian, with the first extension to Bodley's library, the 'Arts End' (1610-12), above. To the west of the Divinity School are the new Convocation House and the Chancellor's Court, both built 1634-7. Above them is the 'Selden End' of the Bodleian, named after the famous lawyer and orientalist John Selden (died 1654), who gave the library a valuable collection of books and manuscripts.

The Proscholium and Arts End form most of the west range of the **Schools Quadrangle** (1613-24; it was begun on the day of Bodley's funeral). The middle floor was designed for the library, the rest being intended for the schools. The most striking feature of the quad is the flamboyant tower (**16**). Painted over the doors round the quad are the names of the schools to which they gave access; lectures and examinations were held here until the 19th century, when the sharp rise in undergraduate numbers led to the building of the grandiose Examination Schools (1882) between Merton Street and the High Street, to

▲ **15** *A sample of the Bodleian Library's rich collection of fine bindings: the embroidered cover of a New Testament (Douce Bib NT Eng. 1625 g.I) made in 1625, supposedly from a waistcoat belonging to Charles I, who used Oxford as his headquarters during the Civil War. On the right King David plays his harp, surrounded by birds, beasts and insects; on the left the angel prevents Abraham from sacrificing Isaac*

►**16** *The Schools Quadrangle: the tower of the five orders, so called because each tier has one of the five classical orders of columns – looking upwards, Tuscan, Doric, Ionic, Corinthian and Composite. On the penultimate tier James I hands copies of his works to Fame and to the University; at the top is the royal coat of arms. In the foreground is a bronze statue (with a rotatable head) of the 3rd Earl of Pembroke, the University's Chancellor 1617-30, attributed to Charles I's sculptor, Le Sueur*

designs by Sir Thomas Jackson. The Bodleian now occupies the whole quad, its most recent major extension being the New Bodleian on the far side of Broad Street, a boring but suitably reticent design by Sir Giles Gilbert Scott (1937).

By the 17th century many churchmen felt that St Mary's should not house noisy secular University ceremonies, and the Chancellor, Archbishop Sheldon, financed the building of a theatre for such functions. The **Sheldonian Theatre** (1663-9), designed by the young Christopher Wren, was Oxford's first classical building; Wren took its unusual D-shape from designs of Roman theatres (**19**). The exterior is enriched with much fine carving, and the present cupola (larger than Wren's original), which was added in 1838, gives excellent views over central Oxford. Wren's contemporaries admired the technical *tour de force* by which he erected a ceiling 21.5 m x 24.5 m without any of the load-bearing columns that would have spoilt spectators' views of ceremonies. His ingenious system of trusses was replaced in the 18th century. Roman theatres were roofless, so Robert Streeter's allegorical painting on the ceiling depicts an open sky, with gilded rope-like divisions simulating the netting which would have supported a canopy. This portrayal of the triumph of Religion, Arts and Science over Envy, Hatred and Malice aroused considerable enthusiasm in its day, one poet remarkably claiming that 'Future Ages must confess they owe / To Streeter more than Michelangelo.' The theatre also contains much superb contemporary woodwork, notably the Chancellor's throne and the two orators' pulpits. The University still holds its major ceremonies here: undergraduates matriculate and receive their degrees, and every June, at the 'Encaenia', the University commemorates its benefactors and bestows honorary degrees on famous people (**78**). On this occasion in 1733 Handel played the organ for the first performance of his oratorio *Athalia*, and in term-time concerts are still given here. On the railings outside the Sheldonian is a series of carved heads, popularly known as 'the Emperors', but probably meant by Wren to recall antique boundary marks (herms). They have twice been replaced, in 1867 and 1972.

The Sheldonian was also intended as a home for the University's printing works, but the presses were in a totally dark basement and the compositors had to move out every time the theatre was required for a ceremony. However, between 1702 and 1704 Oxford University Press published its first bestseller, Clarendon's *History of the Great Rebellion*, and although the Vice-Chancellor embezzled the proceeds of the first two editions, succeeding profits enabled the University to erect a new home for the Press – the solemn and beautiful **Clarendon Building** (1711-15; **17**), designed by Wren's greatest pupil, Hawksmoor. The history of printing in Oxford goes back to 1478. The University was closely involved, but did not itself receive a charter to publish books until 1636, and its press was haphazardly run until 1666, when it was taken over and technically well equipped by Samuel Fell, the tyrannical dean of Christ Church. Expanding business necessitated the move in 1827 to large new premises in Walton Street, an impressive classical building designed by Daniel Robertson. The Clarendon Building is still used for meetings of the Delegates of the Press, the University committee which directs its affairs. The Oxford dictionaries, bibles and books of verse have perhaps done most to make OUP famous throughout the world.

At the time of the Restoration, Oxford was the centre of scientific activity in England. It was here that the men who were to form the nucleus of the Royal Society first gathered. An architectural reminder of this revival is the beautiful

Old Ashmolean Museum (1678-83; **18**), built to house the curiosities presented to the University in 1677 by Elias Ashmole. The miscellaneous collection, which Ashmole had inherited from the son of its assembler, John Tradescant, contained antiquarian coins, books and engravings, and geological and zoological specimens – including the stuffed body of the last dodo to be seen in Europe (by 1755 this had become rather moth-eaten and the University authorities had it burnt; its head and a claw were saved and are now in the University Museum). The Ashmolean was envisaged as a home for experimental science in Oxford and included a chemical laboratory in its basement; it was the University's museum of natural science until its scientific specimens were transferred to the new University Museum in the 19th century. The remaining antiquarian collections were moved in 1894 to the University Galleries in Beaumont Street, built in 1845 to house the University's pictures and the Arundel Marbles (the celebrated group of classical sculpture assembled by the earl of Arundel in the early 17th century). Thus the **Ashmolean Museum of Art and Antiquities** came into being. The building, whose east end also houses the Taylorian Institute, endowed in 1788 for the teaching of modern languages, was designed by C. R. Cockerell; it is one of the last buildings in the classical style to be erected in Oxford. The Ashmolean is one of the most important museums in the country, renowned for its outstanding collections of coins, watches, silver and antiquities of Greece, Rome and Egypt;

▲**20** *The Alfred Jewel, possibly a brooch, in the Ashmolean Museum: an outstanding example of Anglo-Saxon crafts-manship in gold, rock-crystal and enamel, found near the site of Alfred the Great's fortress at Athelney, Somerset. According to the inscription round the edge it was made for the king – who was for long regarded as the University's founder*

▶**21** *The Botanic Garden: the entrance archway (1632-3) by Nicholas Stone, bearing portraits of (left) Charles I, (right) Charles II and (top) the garden's creator, Henry Danvers, Earl Danby*

OVERLEAF ►

22 (left) *The Radcliffe Camera (1737-49), seen from St Mary's tower with (left) the Sheldonian Theatre's cupola and (right) All Souls College*

23 (right) *The University Museum (1855-60): a giraffe gazes up at the dinosaur Iguanadon bernissartensis. Like London's great railway stations this building testifies to the Victorians' belief that glass and cast iron were materials worthy of great architecture. In 1860 it was the scene of the famous debate on evolution in which Huxley, championing Darwin, triumphed over the scoffing of the bishop of Oxford*

for many of the finest drawings by Raphael and Michelangelo in existence; for major paintings by Uccello, Piero di Cosimo, Giorgione, Tiepolo and Claude amongst hundreds of others; for numerous works by Samuel Palmer, Pissarro and the Pre-Raphaelites; and for a large display of Dutch still-lifes. In 1935 the Old Ashmolean, having served as the offices of the compilers of the Oxford English Dictionary, became the Museum of the History of Science, housing thousands of scientific instruments presented to the University by Dr Lewis Evans, including the largest collection of astrolabes in the world.

The other major monument to reawakened scientific activity in Oxford during the 17th century is the earliest **Botanic Garden** in the country. It was created in 1621 by Henry Danvers, Earl Danby, and was at first called the Physic Garden, being devoted to the growing of herbs and plants for medicine. Here in the 1690s the yellow Oxford ragwort was first propagated in this country, from seeds from Mt Etna; it has since spread all over England. Tucked away beside the river and below Magdalen's bell-tower, the garden is one of the most lovable corners of Oxford (**21**, **42**).

Dr Radcliffe, one of the University's greatest benefactors, died in 1714 leaving £40,000 to build a new library, for which land was acquired between St Mary's and the Schools Quad. The **Radcliffe Camera** (**22**) was built between 1737 and 1749. The idea of a circular library on this site was Hawksmoor's, but the architect was James Gibbs, who also designed the Senate House at Cambridge and St Martin-in-the-Fields in Trafalgar Square, London. Often claimed as his masterpiece, the Camera completes the superb architectural ensemble of Radcliffe Square. Originally it housed the Radcliffe Science Li-

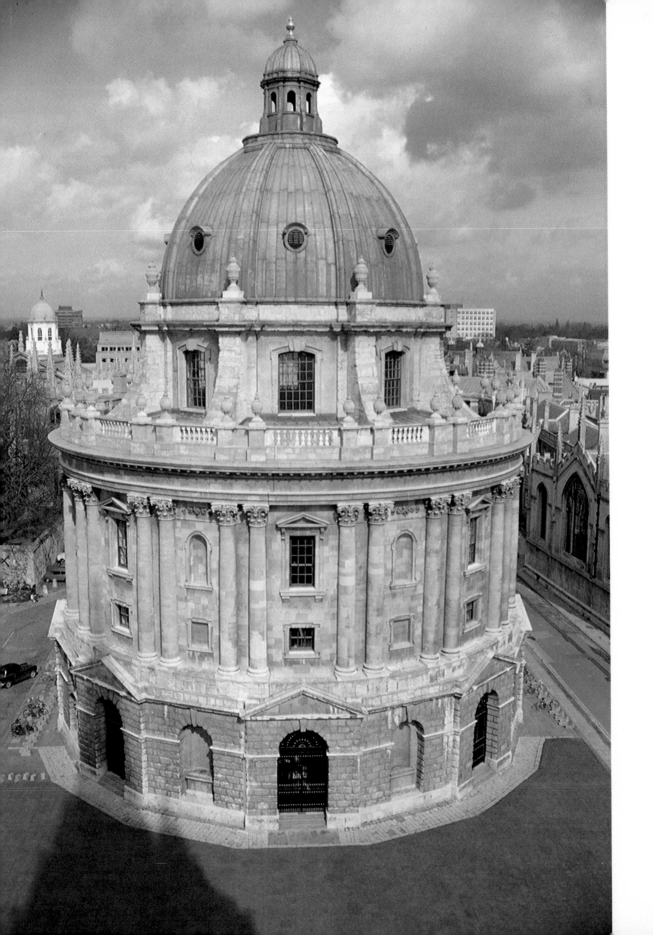

brary, since moved to the science area south of the Parks, and now it is a reading room of the Bodleian.

Radcliffe also financed the unique **Observatory** (**75**), begun in 1772 to a design by Henry Keene and completed in 1794 by Wyatt, who topped it with a version of the Tower of the Winds in Athens. No longer an observatory, it is now part of Green College (see p. 90).

Mid-19th-century educational reforms in Oxford introduced new subjects to the curriculum and necessitated large-scale building of laboratories and lecture rooms. Many of the richer colleges provided their own, but increasingly the responsibility for facilities for scientific teaching and research devolved upon the University. The **University Museum** (1855-60), the first architectural expression of the renewed enthusiasm for the sciences, was the inspiration of Dr Henry Acland, reader in anatomy, who conceived of a museum containing 'all the materials explanatory of the organic being placed upon the globe'. A competition for its design was won by Benjamin Woodward, whose Victorian Gothic structure was strongly advocated by Acland's friend Ruskin. The building demonstrates Ruskin's belief in the importance of the individual craftsman who takes Nature as his model, but much of its decoration remains unfinished because the University meanly withheld the necessary funds. Nevertheless, the interior, a single triple-aisled room surrounded by a gallery, provides one of Oxford's great architectural experiences (**23**). The materials and decoration deliberately reflect the Museum's educational purposes: much of the carving was copied directly from specimens brought from the Botanic Garden, and each column is made from a different stone. The former Chemistry Laboratory to the

▼ **24** *The Law, English and Economics Faculties, designed by Sir Leslie Martin and widely regarded as the University's most distinguished 20th-century building*

▲**25** *Oxford's famous skyline (seen here from Carfax Tower) inspired Matthew Arnold's description in 'Thyrsis' of 'that sweet city with her dreaming spires' and Gerard Manley Hopkins' more accurate evocation of the 'Towery city' in 'Duns Scotus's Oxford'. Left to right: the tower of the Schools Quadrangle, New College bell-tower, the dome of the Radcliffe Camera, the towers of All Souls College (and the new Radcliffe Infirmary in the far distance), St Mary's spire and All Saints' Church*

south of the Museum, modelled on the Abbot's Kitchen at Glastonbury, is part of the original design.

In 1885-6 the **Pitt Rivers Museum** was added to house the vast collection of ethnographical material formed by Lieutenant-General Augustus Pitt Rivers. The distinctive feature of this tightly packed museum is its classification of objects by use, not geographical origin (in accordance with the donor's wishes), demonstrating the evolutionary progress of a particular idea through many different cultures. Thus it is possible to find, in one case, mummies from Egypt and Peru side by side with Burmese Buddhas and images of Christ from medieval Brittany.

The University Museum was the beginning of the science area, a muddle of laboratories, libraries and lecture rooms on the southern edge of the Parks. They include the New Clarendon Laboratory (1948), famous for its work in the development of low-temperature physics. Here helium was first liquefied in this country, and Francis Simon worked on the formulation of the Nernst heat theorem, which became the third law of thermodynamics. In the Pathology Building (1926, with additions 1967-9) H. W. Florey developed the curative properties of penicillin, first used medically in the Radcliffe Infirmary in 1941. New science buildings between the Banbury Road and Keble Road are dominated by the Nuclear Physics Laboratory (1967), whose huge fan-shaped particle accelerator has become one of Oxford's most distinctive landmarks. More pleasing is the Zoology and Psychology Building on the corner of St Cross Road, designed by Sir Leslie Martin in 1965. The same architect was responsible for the building which houses the libraries of the law, English and economics faculties (1961-4; **24**) and for the University offices (1969-73) in Little Clarendon Street, the administrative centre of the University.

3 The Colleges

All Souls College

The first Oxford colleges were societies of graduates; it was not until the 16th century that it became common for them to admit undergraduates. All Souls alone has preserved its medieval character as an exclusively graduate society. It was founded in 1437 by Henry Chichele, archbishop of Canterbury, to support scholars and to serve as a chantry, where prayers would be offered daily for the souls of Henry V and all those who had fallen in battle during the Hundred Years' War. Henry VI accepted the title of co-founder.

The simple and intimate Front Quad (1438-43) has remained virtually unchanged (its High Street frontage was restored 1826-7). The chapel was closely modelled on the chapel at New College, of which Chichele was a member. It too survives largely intact, retaining its splendid hammer-beam roof ornamented with gilded angels, 42 of its original stalls, and medieval stained glass in the four eastern windows of the ante-chapel. 16th-century reformers destroyed many of the other fittings, including the organ, which has never been replaced. The reredos statues were smashed and their niches plastered over. The east wall was twice painted – in 1664 with a Last Judgement by Isaac Fuller ('too full of nakeds for a college chapel', wrote John Evelyn), fragments of which are preserved in the ante-chapel, and in 1713 by Thornhill, who also remodelled the grey and gold classical screen of 1664. In 1870 the reredos was restored and new statues installed; the medieval canopies retain traces of their original bright paint.

For most of the 16th and 17th centuries the college had a reputation for corruption and debauchery, for the fellows often sold their fellowships to the highest bidder. There were occasional brawls, some associated with the cult of the mallard, the most bizarre of all Oxford's traditions. When the college's foundations were being dug a mallard flew out of an ancient drain, an event Chichele had foreseen in a dream. The bird is celebrated in a song at college gaudies (reunion dinners), and in the first year of every century the fellows, carrying staves and torches and a dead duck on a pole, and led by a 'Lord Mallard' carried in a sedan chair, process around the college, singing, drinking and looking for the mallard.

In 1703 a fellow, Dr George Clarke – an amateur architect responsible for much of Worcester College – gained permission to build himself a house on All Souls' ground, to revert to the college on his death. He cleared a site to the north of Front Quad, demolishing the college's medieval cloister, but the house was eventually erected to the east of the old college, on the High Street; since 1736 it

◄ 26 All Souls College: the towers, seen from Queen's Lane, with the dome of the Radcliffe Camera visible between them. The wall on the left is part of the Queen's College

has been the Warden's Lodging. The fellows meanwhile decided to build a new quad on the site of the cloister and asked Hawksmoor to draw up plans. In 1710 Christopher Codrington, a fellow and Governor of the West Indies who had made his fortune in the sugar trade, left the college a large legacy to purchase books and erect a library. As a result the building schemes became more ambitious. Hawksmoor's design is cunning: Gothic on the outside (to harmonise with the chapel) but wholly classical within. The hall, to the east of the chapel, was rebuilt (1729-33), and the Codrington Library (completed 1756) was placed on the opposite side of the new quad. The east range includes the Common Room, and the famous fanciful twin towers which from a distance appear to have been cut from paper (**26**). The low arcade on the west side affords a superb view of the Radcliffe Camera and St Mary's from the quad. On the library is a sun-dial, moved there from the south side of the chapel, where it was erected 1658-9. Christopher Wren was the bursar at that time, and he probably designed it.

The reforms which altered the University in the 19th century left All Souls' graduate character untouched but prompted higher academic standards. Prize fellowships were instituted in 1881; they are competed for by Oxford's cleverest graduates. Since 1966 the college has elected 12 visiting fellows a year, strengthening its modern reputation as a pre-eminent centre of learning and research. All Souls did not open its fellowships to women until 1979.

Balliol College

In 1255 John of Balliol, one of the most powerful and ambitious men in the north of England, came into open dispute with the bishop palatine of Durham over land each claimed as his own. The bishop excommunicated some of Balliol's followers, who he claimed had dispossessed him of the land, and in revenge Balliol ambushed the bishop, assaulted him and kidnapped part of his retinue. The bishop, with the king's support, demanded reparation. Balliol submitted, apparently with good grace (perhaps because he kept most of the disputed land). He went in penance to Durham Cathedral, where he was publicly scourged. He was also required to perform an act of charity, so he hired a house in Oxford near the Church of St Mary Magdalen and converted it into a hostel for 16 poor scholars, each of whom was given a daily allowance of 8d. Although the group of scholars was in existence by 1266, it received no endowments or statutes until 1282, when they were provided by Balliol's widow, Dervorguilla.

Even with her support, the college was poor and remained so for centuries. This was partly intentional: the Balliols' charity was not to provide sinecures, so the statutes debarred anyone earning more than £5 a year from holding a fellowship. Poverty and smallness meant that Balliol played an unimportant role in the medieval University, although the reformer Wyclif, whose heretical teachings greatly damaged Oxford's reputation, was master *c*1360-1. The college received new statutes in 1507, drafted by Bishop Fox, the founder of Corpus Christi College. These made Balliol a theological seminary: for the next 300 years the college was chiefly concerned with educating future clergymen, although there were some famous exceptions, such as John Evelyn, the diarist, who entered Balliol in 1637, and Adam Smith, the economist (at Balliol 1740-6).

► **27** *Balliol College's Broad Street frontage, designed by Sir Alfred Waterhouse, with the college flag flying*

Balliol could not afford ambitious buildings for many years. Front Quad was not finished until the 15th century, and of this only the west range (including the former hall) and part of the north range (the library) survive. Garden Quad was begun in 1594; it contains some attractive 18th- and early-19th-century architecture, notably Fisher Buildings (1767), which are haunted by the lamenting ghost of an 18th-century fellow.

The college's appearance is largely Victorian – appropriately enough, for in the 19th century it rose to unprecedented fame at the forefront of the reforms in education and scholarship. It made every effort to raise its academic standards, introducing series of regular college lectures, an entrance examination and termly 'collections' (tests), which set a pattern for the other colleges. The man chiefly responsible for this was Benjamin Jowett (fellow 1838, master 1870). A translator of Plato, populariser of Greek philosophy and brilliant teacher, he proclaimed a desire 'to inoculate the world with Balliol': he believed that education should prepare a man for a life of action, a novel idea in his time. He did much to enlarge the range of studies, particularly in the sciences. So complete was his domination that undergraduates of the day sang 'Here come I, my name is Jowett; / There's no knowledge but I know it . . .' Largely because of his enthusiasm Balliol produced more eminent Victorians than any other college. They included Matthew Arnold, the critic and poet (many of whose best-known poems, such as 'Thyrsis' and 'The Scholar Gypsy', celebrate Oxford and its surrounding countryside); his poet friend A. H. Clough; the poets Swinburne and Gerard Manley Hopkins; and the statesmen Curzon, Grey and Asquith.

Most of Balliol's buildings date from Jowett's time. The chapel (1856-7) was designed by Butterfield, the architect of Keble, to replace a 16th-century structure. After its exciting red and buff striped exterior, the interior is rather a disappointment, because in 1937 timid dons had Butterfield's lavish decorations removed. There is some beautiful 17th-century panelling at the east end (obscured by the opulent modern metal altar front) and the windows have remnants of 16th-century stained glass. The Broad Street frontage (**27**) was rebuilt in a bold but uningratiating fashion by Sir Alfred Waterhouse, who also designed a new hall (1876-7) at the north end of Garden Quad (now cramped between new buildings designed by the Oxford Architects Partnership). The hall unusually contains a large organ, given by Jowett, to be used for the regular Balliol Sunday evening concerts, which are still a famous Oxford institution.

The high intellectual standards set by Jowett were maintained in the 20th century. The brothers Julian and Aldous Huxley were undergraduates here, as were the novelists L. P. Hartley and Graham Greene, Harold Macmillan (Prime Minister 1957-63 and from 1960 the University's Chancellor), and Lord Peter Wimsey.

Brasenose College

Brasenose College is a descendant of Brasenose Hall (first recorded in 1279), which formerly occupied part of the same site. 'Brasenose', a corruption of 'Brazen Nose', referred to the Hall's original door knocker. In 1890 a house in Stamford came up for sale; the college bought it for the sake of its 13th-century knocker, believed by the fellows to have been stolen from the door of Brasenose Hall in 1333, and this now hangs behind high table in the college dining hall.

The college was founded in 1509 by William Smyth, bishop of Lincoln, and

▲ 28 *Brasenose College:
the cloister (1657-9) and,
above it, the library
(completed 1664)*

Richard Sutton, a lawyer; the reasons for their co-operation are not certain.
Sutton acquired the site and the bishop paid for the buildings, which were
begun at once. The college's early years were rather unsettled. The first bursar,
Roland Messynger, was expelled: his failings are now forgotten but were
considered so great at the time that for centuries new fellows of Brasenose had to
swear not to admit him within the college walls for more than one day. William
Sutton, the lecturer responsible for undergraduates, spent most of his time in
taverns and was eventually dismissed for attacking the constables of Chipping
Norton with a bow and arrow in defence of his mistress' reputation.

   The original chapel stood west of the dining hall in the south range of Old
Quad. It was intended to be temporary, but work did not start on a new chapel
until 1656. This forms the south range of Chapel Quad, which incorporates in
its west range the college's 15th-century kitchen, the only surviving building of
Brasenose Hall. To the east is the library, over an extraordinary cloister with
oval windows, which formed a covered walk and burial ground until it was
unfortunately converted into chambers in 1807 (**28**). The interior of the chapel
is remarkable for its spectacular plaster pendant fan vaulting of 1665. John
Jackson, the master mason, was probably responsible for the design – he also
worked on Canterbury Quad at St John's, from which the idea of a library
above a cloister may have been derived.

   Hawksmoor and Soane were amongst the architects who drew up plans for a
third quad; it was eventually built between 1886 and 1909 to designs by Sir
Thomas Jackson, the architect of the Examination Schools, in his least re-
barbative style. He gave the college an attractive frontage onto the High Street.

Squeezed behind Jackson's quad is Powell and Moya's beautiful building of 1959 containing undergraduate accommodation, the model for their later work at Christ Church.

Christ Church

Christ Church is Oxford's grandest college. It has the largest quad (80.5 m x 79.5 m), the biggest pre-Victorian hall and its own art gallery; its chapel is Oxford Cathedral. This reflects the ambitious concept of Thomas Wolsey, cardinal, Lord Chancellor and the most powerful man in the kingdom. However, four years after founding Cardinal College in 1525 Wolsey fell, having displeased his master, Henry VIII, by his failure to obtain the annulment of the king's marriage to Katharine of Aragon. In 1532 the king rather grudgingly refounded the college as King Henry VIII's College, but subsequently, fired with enthusiasm for learning (which led him also to found Trinity College, Cambridge), he created Christ Church, uniting the college with the cathedral in a single foundation (1546). Its Latin title, Aedes Christi (House of Christ), explains why this most palatial of colleges is often referred to domestically as 'The House'.

For a century Christ Church remained much as Wolsey had left it. The site is that of the dissolved Priory of St Frideswide. Wolsey intended a huge new quad to replace all the priory buildings. His plans for a massive chapel were unrealised, and the old priory church became the college chapel (from 1546 Oxford Cathedral) – a fortunate survival. It dates from 1194: despite later

► **30** *Christ Church: Tom Tower. The upper part, designed by Wren, was added to the gate built in the time of the founder, Cardinal Wolsey. Wolsey's statue was placed over the gate in 1872. In the foreground are (left) St Aldate's Church and (right) Pembroke College. No saint called Aldate is known to have existed; the name is probably a corruption of 'Old Gate', after the city's South Gate, which Wolsey demolished to make way for his college*

▼ **29** *Christ Church: the the 17th-century fan vaulting over the hall staircase, designed by one 'Smith, an artificer of London'*

accretions, the interior appears almost totally Norman, thanks to Victorian restoration. The exception is the vaulting in the chancel, one of the glories of English architecture. This intricate pendant lierne vault (installed *c*1500) is so reminiscent of the vaulting in the Divinity School that it seems likely that the same designer, William Orchard, was responsible for it; he is buried in the cathedral. The bell-chamber and the spire (one of the earliest in England) were erected at the beginning of the 13th century (**31**). The cathedral contains some fine 17th-century woodwork, notably the oak pulpit and the Vice-Chancellor's throne, and several beautiful windows designed by Burne-Jones. The choir is world famous. The dual nature of Henry's foundation meant that the dean and chapter of the cathedral were also the college's governors. The fellows (still known today as 'Students') were mere employees, without the authority enjoyed by fellows in other colleges – a position not altered until 1867.

The cloister and the 13th-century chapter house are the most distinctive survivors of the other priory buildings. Wolsey added the hall, the kitchens and the west front, but left the quad three-sided and its great gate unfinished. The spectacularly fan-vaulted roof of the hall staircase (**29**) was commissioned by Dean Samuel Fell *c*1640, and after the Civil War Fell's son John (dean 1660-86) completed the quad, continuing the vestigial arches and pillars of Wolsey's projected cloister to give the fourth side a uniform appearance. In 1681 Fell commissioned Sir Christopher Wren to finish Wolsey's gateway, which he did with great panache in the form of a massive domed tower (**30**). The bell 'Great Tom' was moved here from the cathedral steeple, and has given its name to the tower and the quad. Every night at 5 past 9 (9 o'clock on the Oxford meridian,

▲**31** *The wide expanse of Christ Church meadow affords magnificent views of the colleges that border it (see also **51**). Left to right: Christ Church: the pinnacles on the hall, Bodley's bell-tower, Tom Tower and the spire and chancel of Oxford Cathedral, which is also Christ Church's chapel (the rose window was installed in 1853); Corpus Christi College: the Fellows' Building (1706-16); and Merton College: the Grove Building*

OVERLEAF ►

Corpus Christi College
33 (left) *The early-16th-century paved Front Quad with its unusual sun-dial on a pillar in the centre. The gate-tower was originally the President's Lodging*
34 (right) *The 18th-century cloister in Fellows' Quad, with memorial tablets to college fellows on the walls*

and formerly the time when the gates were shut) it tolls 101 times; this signifies the 100 scholars of the original foundation plus a studentship added in 1663.

Christ Church had considerable academic standing in the 16th century: the poet Sir Philip Sidney, the composer John Taverner and the geographer Richard Hakluyt all studied here. But despite notable alumni in later centuries, such as the philosopher John Locke, it soon acquired a reputation, which it has never entirely lost, for housing the idle sons of the aristocracy (such as Sebastian Flyte of *Brideshead Revisited*).

Peckwater Quad, on the site of the former Peckwater Inn, was designed by Dean Aldrich and completed in 1713: it is an unusually restrained classical structure for its date. The library (1717-72) on the fourth side was completely refaced in 1960-2, preserving the original rather sickly contrast between white and buff stones (**32**). The lower floor, initially intended to be an arcade, was fitted up in 1764 as a gallery to display the pictures bequeathed to his college by General John Guise. This collection has since been greatly enlarged: as well as important Italian paintings it contains about 1700 outstanding old master drawings, and is now housed in a new gallery (1964-7) by Powell and Moya.

Canterbury Quad (1773-83) stands on the site of the former Canterbury College (founded 1363). Built by Wyatt and financed by Richard Robinson, archbishop of Armagh, it has a beautiful 'triumphal arch' which forms the back gate of the college on Oriel Square.

Many of the most attractive features of Christ Church are Victorian additions, notably the hall pinnacles and the belfry tower over the hall staircase, designed by Bodley. The academic reputation of the college rose during this period, largely through the efforts of Dean Liddell, whose statue can be seen on Fell Tower – which he completed – between Tom Quad and Peckwater.

▼**32** *Christ Church: the library (1717-72), designed by Dr George Clarke of All Souls, who also designed much of Worcester College*

Liddell's daughter Alice inspired Lewis Carroll who, under his real name, Charles Dodgson, taught mathematics at Christ Church. He first told the story that became *Alice in Wonderland* to Alice and her two sisters during a boating expedition to Godstow on 4 July 1862.

Christ Church's alumni have included 18 English Prime Ministers. In 1837 Ruskin began his association with Oxford as a Christ Church undergraduate; he was constantly shadowed by his devoted mother, who hired rooms in the High Street to be near him. Meadow Buildings (1863), an oppressive block of undergraduate accommodation between the college and Christ Church meadows, shows the influence of Ruskin's passionate admiration of Venetian Gothic. In the 20th century Christ Church undergraduates have included the writers Harold Acton and Jan (James) Morris, the composer Sir William Walton and the poet W. H. Auden, who returned here in 1972 to live in a cottage in the grounds. The handsome Blue Boar Quad, designed by Powell and Moya, was built in 1968.

Corpus Christi College

In 1512 Richard Fox, bishop of Winchester and secretary and Lord Privy Seal to both Henry VII and Henry VIII, began to have buildings erected for a new monastic college. However, foreseeing the dissolution of the monasteries, he changed his mind and decided on a secular institution instead, recording in the statutes of 1517 how he 'founded . . . a certain bee garden, which we have named the College of Corpus Christi, wherein scholars, like ingenious bees, are by day and night to make wax to the honour of God . . .' A distinctive feature of these statutes (apart from their pervasive apicultural imagery) is their provision for professors of Latin and Greek who would deliver lectures to the whole University, and their enumeration of the classical writers on whom the professors were to concentrate. This reflects Oxford's reception of Renaissance classical scholarship, which had rapidly become an accepted part of the curriculum. In fact Fox was interested not so much in classical scholarship as in creating a college that could produce educated clergymen. Nevertheless, he established the well-stocked college library, which earned enthusiastic praise from one of the greatest scholars of the Renaissance, Erasmus.

Front Quad (**33**) was largely complete when the college was founded in 1517. In the centre stands the famous sun-dial, set up in 1581. A perpetual calendar was painted on the pillar in 1605. At the top is a statue of a pelican in her piety, the emblem of Corpus Christi (it was once thought that the pelican fed her young with blood pecked from her own breast, and this was interpreted as an image of Christ's blood sustaining the faithful). The chapel has simple pleasing woodwork (17th century) and a brass lectern of 1537 in the shape of a melancholy eagle. The Fellows' Building of 1706-16, perhaps designed by Dean Aldrich of Christ Church, looks onto the college's pretty garden and Christ Church meadows beyond. The building forms one side of the Fellows' Quad (the smallest quad in Oxford) opposite a cloister of the same date (**34**).

Corpus is famous for its collection of gold and silver plate, which it managed to preserve during the Civil War despite Charles I's request that all the colleges surrender their plate to him to be melted down. Corpus gave money instead, and was allowed to redeem its treasures, which include the founder's elaborate golden pastoral staff.

► **35** *Exeter College: a view of George Gilbert Scott's chapel of 1856, modelled on the Sainte-Chapelle, across the rooftops of Brasenose College. The Old Quad of Brasenose is in the foreground; the sun-dial was erected in 1719*

Exeter College

Exeter College is the creation of Walter Stapledon, bishop of Exeter, who in 1314 gave the dean and chapter of Exeter Cathedral a rectory, instructing them to use the income from it to support 12 scholars at Oxford. For many centuries the college had a special connection with Devon and Cornwall.

The only surviving medieval building is the former main entrance, Palmer's Tower (1432), opposite the east end of the chapel. It is named after William Palmer, rector (i.e. master) 1425-32. The present main gate of the college, on Turl Street, was built in the 18th century and given its present Gothic appearance in 1833. At the beginning of the 17th century Sir John Acland, dismayed by the squalid and overcrowded condition of the college, financed the building of a new dining hall (1618). This has a splendid screen of the same date and a porch and fireplaces designed by John Nash (1820). The 17th-century chapel was demolished in 1856 to make way for one designed by George Gilbert Scott, which he loosely modelled on the Sainte-Chapelle in Paris. Far too big for its surroundings, the new chapel is a typical and enjoyable piece of high-Victorian self-confidence. The memorable interior is lavishly decorated with mosaic, brass and wrought iron. Its fittings include stalls by Bodley, a stone screen and organ gallery, and a large William Morris tapestry, *The Adoration of the Kings*, designed by Burne-Jones. Morris and Burne-Jones became undergraduates at Exeter in 1853, both intending to enter the Church; but inspired by Ruskin, Rossetti and the medieval splendours of Oxford they rejected conventional careers and dedicated themselves to art.

George Gilbert Scott also designed a new library overlooking the tree-filled Fellows' Garden. North of the chapel is Margary Quad, which includes the Thomas Wood building (1964) designed by Brett and Pollen. Exeter's 20th-century undergraduates have included the actor Richard Burton and J. R. R. Tolkien, the author of *The Hobbit* and *The Lord of the Rings* and professor of Anglo-Saxon.

Hertford College

Hertford College has a complicated history. Its site and some of its buildings are those of Hart Hall, one of the many halls accommodating students in the Middle Ages, which is first recorded in 1301 as existing on land belonging to Elias de Hertford – hence its name. In 1312 it was bought by Walter Stapledon, the founder of Exeter College, and remained in that college's possession for centuries. Hart Hall had a number of distinguished members, including the poets Samuel Daniel and John Donne. Dr Richard Newton, who was principal at the beginning of the 18th century, was eager to transform Hart Hall into a college – as Gloucester Hall had been transformed into Worcester College – and run it as a model of educational reform. He went so far as to obtain the necessary charter and rename the hall Hertford College, but his plans foundered for lack of adequate endowment. After his death Hertford decayed to the point that it became impossible to find someone to accept the post of principal.

This decline coincided with a fierce conflict between Magdalen College and another academic hall, Magdalen Hall, which had grown up independently of the college in buildings that William of Waynflete, the college's founder, had intended for a grammar school. The college lost its power to appoint the principal of Magdalen Hall in the 17th century, and thereafter it struggled

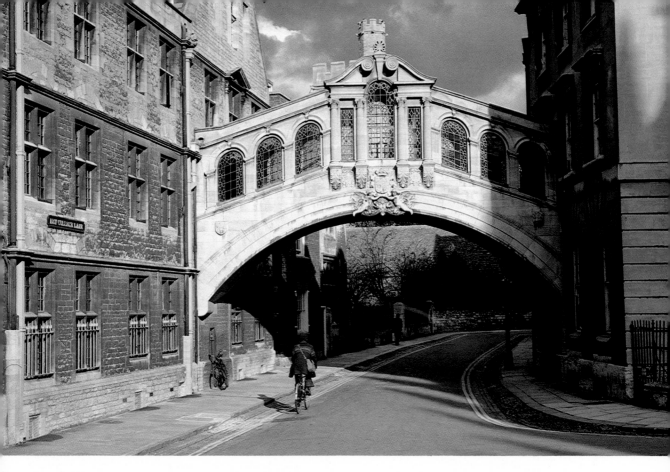

▲**36** *Hertford College: the Bridge of Sighs (1913-14) over New College Lane links Hertford's quads. Sir Thomas Jackson's design resembles the Venetian Bridge of Sighs (which prisoners crossed from the Doge's Palace to the gaol) much more closely than does its Gothic Cambridge counterpart. New College bell-tower is visible behind the bridge*

OVERLEAF ▶

Jesus College
37 (left) *Front Quad (mostly early 17th century) with the spire of Exeter College Chapel behind*

38 (right) *The doorway in Front Quad to the Principal's Lodgings, with its 18th-century shell-hood*

either to regain control or to eject the hall from its land. At the beginning of the 19th century Magdalen's fellows suggested that Hertford College be closed down and its property handed over to the Crown, which could then grant the site and buildings to the University to hold on trust for Magdalen Hall. The plan was successful, and the move was accelerated in 1820 when most of Magdalen Hall's buildings were destroyed by a fire which started after an undergraduate's supper party.

In 1874 Magdalen Hall was refounded as Hertford College with money provided by the banker Thomas Charles Baring. The college was almost entirely rebuilt (1887-9) to designs by Sir Thomas Jackson, including the 'Bridge of Sighs' over New College Lane, which links the college's two quads (**36**). The North Quad contains an octagonal chapel (*c*1520) with the annunciation carved in the lintel of the south doorway.

Hertford's most famous member in modern times was Evelyn Waugh; he was an undergraduate during the 1920s, and in the opening chapter of his first novel, *Decline and Fall*, gives an acid description of Oxford life of that period.

Jesus College

The college was initially founded 'for the maintenance of certain scholars of Wales to be trained up in good letters' by Dr Hugh Price, born Hugh ap Rees in Brecon in *c*1495. Its membership remained largely Welsh until the late 19th century, for most of the benefactions and endowments it received were restricted to Welshmen, and the connection is still strong; until 1925 there were regular chapel services in Welsh. The college's important collection of Welsh manu-

scripts includes the famous 14th-century Llyfr Coch or Red Book of Hergest, containing Welsh legends and romances of King Arthur and Merlin.

At his death in 1574 Price left Jesus College without enough money to finish the buildings he had begun, and completion of the Front Quad (**37**) had to await 17th-century endowments. The chapel was consecrated in 1621. Apart from the late-17th-century screen its internal fittings are mostly Victorian, and now thought to be so offensive that they are curtained from view. In the north-west corner of the quad are the Principal's Lodgings, *c*1625; the attractive shell-hood of the doorway (**38**) is early 18th century. The hall was built *c*1617, the screen with its frieze of Welsh dragons being installed soon afterwards. The barrel-vaulted plaster ceiling was added in 1741. The Inner Quad (1640-1714) has prettily curved gables, similar to those at University College. In Third Quad is a long building on Ship Street (1905), and beyond it is the Old Members' Building (1969-71) containing undergraduate accommodation, a perky design by John Fryman.

The college's many Welsh alumni include Thomas Vaughan, an alchemist and magician, admitted in 1638, and (probably) his twin brother, the poet Henry Vaughan. T. E. Lawrence (Lawrence of Arabia) came here in 1907 from Oxford High School; there is a bust of him by Eric Kennington in the chapel. Harold Wilson (Prime Minister 1964-70, 1974-6) was also a Jesus undergraduate (admitted 1934); the portrait of him in the hall is by Ruskin Spear.

Lincoln College

In 1382 the writings of Wyclif – the first man to translate the Bible into English – were officially condemned, but they continued to circulate within the University, and in the following century Oxford became known as a centre of heresy. To combat this menace Richard Fleming, bishop of Lincoln, founded a college (1427) to train orthodox theologians. His sudden death in 1431, when little more than the gate-tower was built, left Lincoln college poor and incomplete for many years. Front Quad (**40**) was continued by the second founder, John Forest, dean of Wells, in the late 1430s but was not finished until *c*1478. Its picturesque charm is partly due to its having remained two-storied, whereas most medieval quads had a third storey added in the 17th century. The hall retains much of its 15th-century structure, including the original roof with an octagonal louvre – the outlet for smoke from the hearth, which was formerly in the centre of the hall. The screen and wainscotting were installed 1697-1700.

So successful was Fleming in creating an orthodox college that under the 16th-century Protestant rulers it suffered for harbouring too many adherents to the old religion. Its character changed: it ceased to be a seminary, and in the 1560s it began taking undergraduates. This necessitated the erection of a second quad (begun 1608), which includes a new chapel (consecrated 1631) containing outstanding contemporary woodwork; the screen, made of cedar, continued until the 18th century to emit a sweet fragrance. The front stalls, ornamented with statuettes, and the ceiling, bearing coats of arms of college benefactors, date from 1686-7. The stained glass (1629-30) by Bernard van Linge is probably the best of his work in Oxford, the east window of parallel scenes from the Old and New Testaments being particularly rich.

Lincoln's most famous alumnus is John Wesley, the founder of Methodism. He became a fellow in 1726, having graduated at Christ Church, and with his

brother Charles formed a small society – the Holy Club – for worship, Bible study and good works. The leisured and worldly dons of 18th-century Oxford regarded such displays of religious enthusiasm very coldly, and in 1735 Wesley sailed to Georgia. A room in the college, thought to have been his, has been furnished as a memorial and is open to the public. Famous members of the college in the 20th century include Edward Thomas and Osbert Lancaster.

All Saints' Church, adjoining the college, served as the City Church from 1896, when St Martin's at Carfax was demolished, until 1971, when it became Lincoln's library. There has been a church on this site since at least the 12th century; the unusual rotunda and diminutive spire on the tower of the present building (1706-8), designed by Dean Aldrich of Christ Church, are distinctive features of Oxford's skyline (**25**).

Magdalen College

Magdalen (pronounced maudlin) College was founded in 1458 by William of Waynflete, Lord Chancellor of England and bishop of Winchester, on the site of the decayed Hospital of St John, which Henry III had founded in 1233. The new foundation was a large one, including a president, 40 fellows and 30 demies (the college's name for its scholars, derived from the fact that their stipend was half that of the fellows). The prescribed subjects were philosophy and theology, and by 1478 a grammar school had been established to provide a grounding in Latin. Also part of the original foundation was the choir, still one of the finest in Oxford.

Building began in 1467 with the erection of the boundary walls. The architect

▲ **40** *An autumnal view of Lincoln College's 15th-century Front Quad; the sash windows were inserted in the 18th century*

may have been the master mason William Orchard, who probably designed the Divinity School and cathedral chancel vaults. The remains of the 13th-century hospital hall were incorporated into the walls of the kitchens. The cloister, hall and chapel were completed by *c*1510. The bell-tower, Oxford's most famous landmark, is 44 m high and was probably designed by the mason in charge, William Reynolds (**42**). The traditional singing by the choir from the top of the tower, at 6 a.m. every May Day, was originally a prolonged and jolly secular concert; a religious element was introduced in the late 18th century, when the choir adopted the present custom of singing part of the college's Latin grace. Large crowds gather to listen from punts on the river, and the ceremony is followed by bell-ringing and morris dancing.

If any building evokes Matthew Arnold's vision of Oxford 'whispering . . . the last enchantments of the Middle Age' it is Magdalen's cloister, whose history is however surprisingly eventful. In 1822 a number of dons who wanted a view of the chapel and hall from their rooms in the 18th-century New Building instigated the demolition of the entire north range while the rest of the fellows were on holiday, on the pretext that it was too decayed to be repaired. One of the absentees returned unexpectedly, in time to save the remainder, and the demolishing dons were forced to have the range rebuilt to a new design. However, the result was so unbearably hideous that it was again knocked down, this time to be replaced with a copy of the original. The Founder's Tower, dominating the west side of the cloister, was formerly the college's front entrance (**43**). The series of carved figures on the cloister buttresses (**45**), including a pelican, a panther, a dragon and a hippopotamus, and dating from 1509, has often been claimed to have an allegorical significance, but has never been satisfactorily explained.

▼**41** *Magdalen College: the 15th-century High Street frontage, the earliest part of the college buildings, incorporates stonework from the chapel of the Hospital of St John which preceded Magdalen on this site. The well-scrubbed appearance of the masonry is due to recent restoration work, when the carvings of the string-course were renewed (see also* **80**)

The chapel is T-shaped, on the model of Merton and New College Chapels. 32 of the 15th-century stalls, with interesting misericords, are now in the ante-chapel. The reredos was restored in the 19th century; the present vaulting is a copy of the 1790 original. The hall was begun in 1474. The present roof is a 20th-century reproduction of the original, which was removed in 1790. The linen-fold panelling is 16th century, and is said to have come from the dissolved abbey at Reading. Above high table are interesting carvings of Henry VIII and scenes from the life of Mary Magdalene (1541). The screen was installed in 1605 to celebrate a visit by James I.

In the 17th century Magdalen took a leading part in Oxford's opposition to the pro-Catholic policies of James II. When its president died in 1687 the king decided that the college – reputedly the richest in Oxford – should become a Catholic seminary, and ordered it to appoint as its new president a debauched Catholic from Cambridge. The fellows bravely made their own choice; when they refused to reverse it, James installed another protégé, the bishop of Oxford, by force, and had all the most obdurate fellows dismissed. But next year, in fear of William of Orange's imminent invasion, he reinstated them – a victory which the college still celebrates annually with a peal of bells.

New Building (begun 1733; **44**) was probably designed by Dr Clarke of All Souls, the architect of Christ Church Library. It was to be the north side of a large classical quad, a plan which was finally abandoned in the 19th century. Throughout the 18th century the college, like the rest of the University, was leisured and unscholarly. Edward Gibbon, author of *The Decline and Fall of the*

▲46 *Summer in Magdalen Deer Park: fallow deer grazing and resting in the shade*

◄44, 45 *Magdalen College:* (above) *the 18th-century New Building from the water walks;* (below) *the carved figures of a werewolf, hyena, panther, griffin and Anger on the buttresses of the 15th-century cloister*

Roman Empire, recalled that the 14 months that he spent at Magdalen (1752-3) were 'the most idle and unprofitable of my whole life'. The college retained an 18th-century air well into the Victorian era under the venerable Routh, who was president from 1793 until he died, aged 99, in 1854. Thereafter it began to raise its academic standards. New buildings on the site of Magdalen Hall (see under Hertford College) by Bodley and Garner (1880-4), extended by Scott (1928-30), housed the growing number of undergraduates. Bodley's is the four-storey gate-tower opposite the Founder's Tower. Undergraduates in the 19th century included Oscar Wilde (admitted 1874) and his lover, the wicked Lord Alfred Douglas. In 1912 the Prince of Wales, later Edward VIII, became a member of the college. Two well-known members in the 1920s were Sir John Betjeman and Bertie Wooster.

Much of Magdalen's beauty lies in its extensive grounds (**9**, and see map of the river); the college had room to expand because it was outside the city walls. Deer are recorded in the Grove (**46**) as early as 1720. Addison's Walk (16th century), beside the meadows on the far side of the Cherwell, is named after the essayist Joseph Addison (elected demy 1690), who liked to stroll there; other walks were added in the 19th century. The Paddock is famous for its purple and white fritillaries, which flower in April.

Merton College

For centuries the title of Oxford's oldest college has been claimed by Merton, University and Balliol Colleges. Merton received its first statutes in 1264, almost 20 years before the others; Balliol and University date their foundation from their founders' provision of money for the support of scholars in the mid 13th century, but Merton is the earliest organised college.

In 1262 Walter de Merton, Lord Chancellor of England, made over the income from certain of his estates in Surrey to a community of scholars. He bought land in both Oxford and Cambridge, being apparently uncertain where to establish his college. However, in 1270 the scholars were installed in Oxford on land between the city wall and what is now Merton Street. The college remained by far the largest and grandest in Oxford until New College was founded in 1379.

The first building to be specially erected was the hall, which was in existence by 1277. Unfortunately it was extensively remodelled in 1794 and again in 1874. The magnificent chapel took more than 150 years to build; even so it is only a fragment, for the founder intended it to have a long nave, but the choir and transepts, being sufficient for college purposes, were all that was ever built. The first glimpse of the interior, dominated by the lofty arches of the crossing, is breathtaking. The choir was built first (*c*1290-7). Its windows, including the huge and intricate east window, retain their original stained glass – the survival of such a complete sequence is very rare. The crossing dates from 1330-5 and the north and south transepts from 1367 and 1425. The majestic tower was not

▲47 Merton College: the north and east ranges of 14th-century Mob Quad, the oldest quadrangle in the University. The turret in the corner is part of the college's treasury

►48 Merton College: the gateway (1418) onto Merton Street

◄ 49 *Merton College: the 14th-century library (the furnishings, including the desks and bookshelves, are mostly early 17th century). Treasures usually on display include Chaucer's astrolabe, the first printed Bible in Welsh and several books chained to the desks in medieval fashion to prevent theft: in the Middle Ages a book could cost as much as a small farm*

completed until 1450. The chapel's most interesting fittings include a screen designed by Wren (1671) and since much reduced in size, a brass lectern of *c*1500 and a Siberian green marble font presented by Tsar Alexander I in 1816. A monument to Sir Thomas Bodley (1613), founder of the Bodleian Library and fellow of Merton, includes a portrait bust flanked by piles of books. The organ, in pleasure-steamer style, was installed in 1968.

Merton has the oldest quadrangle in Oxford, Mob Quad (**47**; the origin of the name is unknown). It was not designed as a quad, but grew up in that shape by accident. The earliest parts are the east ranges and treasury (1304-7). Most of the upper floor of the south and west ranges is occupied by the library, one of the oldest in England (1371-8; **49**). It is usually open to the public during vacations.

Beautiful additions were made to the college in the 15th century. The main gate-tower was erected in 1418; its Merton Street front bears a carved panel showing John the Baptist in the wilderness, surrounded by rabbits. Over the archway at the east end of the hall are the Lodgings built by Warden Richard Fitzjames in 1497. The horoscope he had cast for his new building reveals that the foundation stone was laid on 12 March at 10.20 a.m. precisely. The vaulting of the arch has 12 bosses carved into the signs of the Zodiac, presumably reflecting Fitzjames' astrological interests. Queen Henrietta Maria lived in the Warden's Lodgings when she held court at Merton during the Civil War.

Fellows' Quad (built 1608-10) incorporates as a centre-piece a tower of four orders, resembling the much larger contemporary tower in the Schools Quad. At the south-west corner of the college, overlooking Christ Church meadows, is the Grove Building (1864), originally designed by William Butterfield but reconstructed in 1930 on the initiative of Merton's dons, who thought it ugly – a philistine act but a suitable revenge on the architect who had wanted to demolish Mob Quad for a new building of his own. Merton possesses the site of St Alban's Hall, one of the four academic halls of the Middle Ages (see p. 6) which survived to the end of the 19th century. It was demolished in 1905 to make way for St Alban's Quad, designed by Basil Champneys.

Sir Max Beerbohm was an undergraduate at Merton (1891-4). His novel *Zuleika Dobson* tells how the entire undergraduate population of Oxford commits suicide for love of the heroine. A room next to the library houses a collection of Beerbohm's cartoons and letters, including many caricatures of contemporary Oxford figures. T. S. Eliot spent a year at Merton (1914-15) after leaving Harvard. Other distinguished members of the college in the 20th century include the poets Edmund Blunden and Louis MacNeice, the novelist Angus Wilson, the composer Lennox Berkeley and the poet Keith Douglas, who came up as an undergraduate in 1938 and was killed in battle six years later.

New College

'New College' was originally the name by which St Mary's College of Winchester was familiarly distinguished from an earlier St Mary's College (now Oriel), but at the time of its foundation (1379) by William of Wykeham, Chancellor of England and bishop of Winchester, it was new in more influential ways as well. It was the first Oxford college to accommodate undergraduates, and the first to be designed on a quadrangle plan (for Mob Quad at Merton had

grown up haphazardly). It was also the first to be faced entirely with dressed stone; the founder was the richest prelate in England, and his college far exceeded in size and wealth any previous foundation at Oxford or Cambridge.

William intended New College to supply the Church with parish priests to make good the heavy losses caused by the Black Death. He also intended it to function as a chantry offering daily prayers for his soul, and to this end provided 10 chaplains, 3 clerks and 16 choristers for the chapel. To this day New College is internationally famous for its choir. To ensure that the students had a thorough early education William made his college a dual foundation with a new grammar school at Winchester – now Winchester College – from which it took all its scholars (providing the model for King's College, Cambridge, which is linked to Eton).

On William's death in 1404 the college was largely complete. The royal charter permitting the foundation, on an extensive site just inside the city walls to the north-east, instructed New College to maintain its section of the wall (then vital to the town's defence). The college complied, and this part of the wall still stands, forming an impressive backdrop to the college gardens (**3**). The college's main entrance is through the gate-tower, the earliest in Oxford, in New College Lane; the upper part is still used as the Warden's Lodgings. Great Quad was erected 1380-6; the addition of a third storey (1674-5) has given it a barrack-like appearance.

Though William may have intended a larger chapel, for which he failed to acquire the land, the present T-shape was soon found to be ideal for college purposes, and was widely imitated in later foundations. The choir was used

▲ **50** *Merton College's Fellows' Quad from Christ Church meadow, with the Radcliffe Camera and the spire of St Mary's behind. The path between the meadow and the college is called Dead Man's Walk, supposedly because a Colonel Windebank was executed here during the Civil War for surrendering the village of Bletchingdon to Parliamentarian forces, but more probably because in the Middle Ages it led to the Jewish cemetery on the site of the Botanic Garden*

▶ **51** *A view down New College Lane from Hertford Bridge, looking towards New College cloister, chapel and bell-tower*

when the whole college worshipped together; the ante-chapel was suitable for private Masses and college meetings, and the fellows still assemble there to elect a new warden. The present hammer-beam roof is Victorian; of the original stalls little remains but the superb set of 62 misericords. The stone statues of the medieval reredos were smashed by reformers in the 16th century and renewed by restorers in the 19th (**77**). Much of the original stained glass was removed by 18th-century improvers, but that in the ante-chapel, apart from the great west window, is 14th century. In 1777 Sir Joshua Reynolds was asked to design new glass for the west window. The finished Nativity with seven virtues underneath, painted by Thomas Jervais, was a bitter disappointment to Reynolds, and most critics have agreed with Walpole that 'Sir Joshua's washy virtues make the Nativity a dark spot'; but the individual parts of the composition have great beauty. The eerie statue of the risen Lazarus below is by Epstein (**54**). To the left of the altar are the founder's gorgeous gilt and enamelled crozier and a painting of St James by El Greco.

The cloister, which was begun in 1390 and retains its original timber roof, was intended for burials and, perhaps, processions on feastdays. It is perfectly complemented by the huge ilex tree in one corner and the bell-tower behind, and evokes an idyllic image of Oxford in the Middle Ages (**52, 53**).

The hall (**76**) was the first in Oxford to be placed back-to-back with the chapel. It retains its 16th-century panelling and screen; the stained glass and the roof are mid Victorian. On feast days in medieval times the older members were permitted, by the college statutes, to amuse their juniors with 'poems,

52, 53 *New College: (above) the 14th-century cloisters and (right) their garden, shaded by the ancient ilex tree; in the centre, above the cloister, can be seen the carving of the founder, Bishop Wykeham, on the outside of the entrance gate*

chronicles of kingdoms and the wonders of this world'. Next to the hall, in the north-east corner of the quad, is the Muniment Tower, for the safekeeping of college valuables. The lower floor is now a museum where the magnificent collection of gold and silver plate is sometimes displayed, with other treasures, such as the founder's mitre and a unicorn's horn.

At the end of the 15th century New College was the centre of humanist learning in Oxford, but thereafter it lapsed into three centuries of idleness and introspection. By the 17th century the fellows had come to dislike living four to a room as the founder had stipulated (so that seniors could look after juniors), and Garden Quad was built (completed 1684) to provide greater comfort. Its unconventional plan was necessitated by the 'Exchequer' (bursary) facing the garden, a 15th-century extension to the original buildings. The architect, William Byrd, constructed an identical block to the south and then two higher narrow wings to the east, set back so as to touch the lower blocks at the corner and thus screening the medieval kitchens and latrines from view. In 1700 two further stepped-back blocks were added to the east of Garden Quad – the first buildings in the University to have sash windows. The quad also includes the first Junior Common Room. The beautiful wrought-iron screen and gate between the quad and the gardens were designed in 1711. The gardens, the finest in Oxford, are dominated by the ancient city walls and by the late-16th-century mound (a common ornamental feature of Elizabethan gardens), known in the 18th century as Parnassus.

In 1834 the college finally surrendered its privilege of claiming degrees for its students without their having taken University examinations, and began to

◀ **54** *New College
Chapel: Epstein's statue
(1951) of Lazarus rising
from the grave*

raise its academic standards, with such success that for long its reputation was second only to Balliol's. In 1854 fellows began to be drawn from schools other than Winchester; in 1866 the first open scholarships were created. Increasing numbers of undergraduates led to the building of new accommodation along Holywell Street, designed by Scott (1872) and Champneys (1896-7). Much of this development was initiated by Dr Spooner (elected warden 1903), who also gave his name to the word 'spoonerism' (but though he did once announce a hymn as 'Kinquering kongs their tikles tate', most of the instances attributed to him are apocryphal). With the erection in Longwall Street of the first accommodation in any of the ancient colleges specifically for graduates (1961-3, designed by David Roberts), New College has continued its tradition of innovation into modern times.

Oriel College

Oriel College is the nickname of the House of the Blessed Mary the Virgin in Oxford, founded in 1326 by Adam de Brome, one of Edward II's civil servants. The name is derived from a tenement which used to stand on the site, called 'La Oriole' presumably because an oriel (an upper floor bay window) was a prominent feature. The king added valuable property and endowments, and the college therefore regards him as its co-founder. Oriel was closely modelled on Merton, and remained a graduate society until the 16th century.

The influx of undergraduates and the poor state of the medieval buildings necessitated complete rebuilding in the years 1620-42. Like University College, which it much resembles, Oriel reflects the influence of Wadham in the symmetry of its buildings and in the grouping of the hall and chapel on the east side of the quad (**55**). To the south, Merton Chapel looms over the prettily shaped gables.

The east and west ranges of Back Quad were built in the 18th century, but faithfully imitate the Gothic style of Front Quad. The north range is James Wyatt's library (1788), a simple harmonious building attractively framed by trees. The gloomy passage to the right of the library leads to St Mary's Quad. Until 1902 this was St Mary's Hall, one of the last surviving academic halls (see p. 6). The buildings, which once formed the rectory of St Mary's Church, were appropriated by Oriel in 1326. The principal of St Mary's was usually a fellow of Oriel, but the hall retained its own distinct identity. St Mary's chapel and dining hall are in the south range (1639-40), one on top of the other. The chapel windows have particularly lovely tracery. The chapel is now Oriel's Junior Library, and the dining hall the Junior Common Room. The west range (1826) is an early example of the Gothic revival, before the style became earnest and academic in the hands of the Victorians. Opposite is a timber-framed house of 1743 and to the north, fronting the High Street, is the Rhodes Building (1909-11), designed by Basil Champneys and named after Cecil Rhodes, who was an undergraduate at Oriel and left the college part of his fortune.

Oriel was famous in the 19th century as the centre of the Oxford Movement (see p. 13): Newman, Pusey, Froude and Keble were all fellows. Sir Walter Raleigh was also a member of Oriel (*c*1572); and the naturalist Gilbert White was a fellow from 1744 to 1793, but he spent most of his time at his lifelong home, Selborne, Hampshire, which he describes in *The Natural History and Antiquities of Selborne*.

55 *Oriel College: the hall porch. The statues are of Edward II and, probably, Charles I. The open-work lettering records that the porch was built in Charles' reign*

Pembroke College

Pembroke College, founded in 1624, is a descendant of Broadgates Hall (first mentioned in 1446). In 1610 and 1623 the University received benefactions for the maintenance at Oxford of fellows and scholars to be drawn from Abingdon School. The school's governors successfully petitioned James I to make Broadgates Hall into a college where the recipients of these benefactions could live. The new college was named after the University Chancellor, the Earl of Pembroke, who helped to draw up its statutes.

The Old Quad (**56**) was built 1626-70 but refaced 1829-30, when the gate-tower was rebuilt. To the west is Chapel Quad, dominated by a picturesque group of ivy-clad 19th-century buildings, including the hall (1848). The chapel was consecrated in 1732. The interior was remodelled in 1884 by C. E. Kempe, and so richly decorated that the walls and ceiling seem to have been carpeted. The stalls and the beautiful screen date from the 1630s. North Quad is an ingenious mixture of a brick building of 1966-7 with a range of old houses in Pembroke Street. To the east of Old Quad is Sir Leslie Martin's new library (opened 1974). Wolsey's almhouses (begun *c*1525), which front St Aldate's, are now the Master's Lodgings.

The most famous member of Pembroke was Samuel Johnson, the critic and lexicographer. Boswell records that 'His apartment . . . was that upon the second floor, over the gateway. The enthusiasts of learning will ever contemplate it with veneration.' He was so poor that he had to leave Oxford after 14 months, without taking a degree (the University later awarded him an honorary doctorate), but he frequently revisited his old college, and left it his library. The college also possesses his teapot and his portrait by Reynolds.

▼56 *Pembroke College: Old Quad, with Christ Church's Tom Tower peering over. The quad is enlivened by its luxuriant foliage and by the inscriptions of the college's victorious oarsmen at the side of the doors*

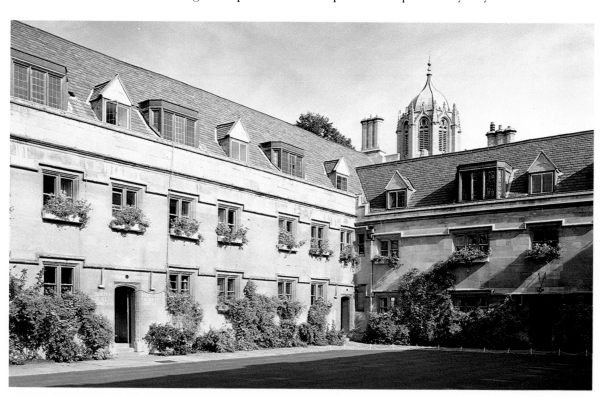

The Queen's College

Because Queen's has one of the most perfect ensembles of 17th- and 18th-century architecture in the country few visitors realise that it is one of Oxford's oldest colleges. It was founded in 1340 by Robert of Eglesfield, chaplain to the wife of Edward III, Queen Philippa, who permitted him to describe her as foundress. The plans were grander than those of any earlier college, but Robert did not have the financial resources to realise them all. Much of the college's organisation was symbolic: there was to be a provost and 12 fellows (commemorating Christ and the apostles), who were to sit on three sides of high table, as at the Last Supper, and wear blood-red robes in memory of Christ's sacrifice. Dinner was to be (and still is) announced by a blast on a silver trumpet, instead of the more usual bell.

Robert died in 1349, perhaps of the Black Death. His memory is preserved in the college by his gift of the horn of an aurochs (the extinct European wild ox), mounted in silver gilt and inscribed 'Wacceyl' ('make merry'), which still serves as a loving-cup at college feasts. The two annual feasts for which Queen's is famous were established soon after the founder's death. The Boar's Head Feast, formerly held on Christmas Day, commemorates Copcot, a student of Queen's who was strolling in Shotover Forest one day when he was attacked by a ferocious boar. He thrust the copy of Aristotle which he had been reading into the boar's mouth. 'Graecum est', exclaimed the boar, and died. At the feast, a decorated boar's head is carried into the hall to the accompaniment of the Boar's Head Carol (composed by an unknown member of Queen's). At the Needle and Thread Dinner the bursar presents each guest with a needle and thread, saying 'Take this and be thrifty' – a custom thought to originate in a French pun, *aiguilles et fils* (needles and threads), on the founder's name.

Building of the original college quad took about 70 years (completed *c*1410); the chapel was not finished until the 16th century. The quad was entered from Queen's Lane (opposite St Edmund Hall), for there was still a row of houses between the college and the High Street. The college's imposing medieval buildings would have been familiar to Wyclif (see p. 10), a member of Queen's (1363-5, 1374-81), and perhaps to Henry V, who may have studied here while Prince of Wales. Today barely a stone of them remains. In 1670 Provost Williamson was shocked to find that a nobleman staying in the college had to share a room with undergraduates, so cramped had accommodation become. He instigated a new range of buildings, partly designed by Wren, and now, in a remodelled form, the east range of North Quad. This was followed (1692-5) by a new library (**58**) to house a large bequest of books. The contrast between this, one of the finest classical buildings in Oxford, and the by now rather dilapidated medieval quad prompted schemes for rebuilding the whole college. Hawksmoor was asked for designs, which he produced in great abundance. None of those that survive corresponds to the final building, the plans of which have been lost, but its architecture is so outstanding as to suggest Hawksmoor's authorship (and to make it hard to regret the loss of the old buildings).

Front Quad, on the High Street, was begun in 1709. The chapel was consecrated in 1719; it has beautiful contemporary woodwork (in particular an elaborate screen) and a sumptuous stucco ceiling which contains, in the apse, an athletic representation of the Ascension by Thornhill. The screen and the gatehouse, fronting the High Street, were completed in 1760 (**57**).

►**57** *The Queen's College: the cupola over the entrance gate on the High Street, designed by Hawksmoor, from the west arcade in Front Quad. The statue is of Queen Caroline, wife of George II, who gave money for rebuilding the college*

58 *The Queen's College Library (1692-5). The ground floor, originally an open arcade, was closed in 1841 to make more room for books. The pediment carvings represent Wisdom and attendant amorini carrying instruments of scholarship; the eagle on a globe above, like the eagles on the college coat of arms, is a canting reference to the founder's name, Eglesfield*

Famous members of Queen's in the 17th century included the playwright Wycherley and Edmund Halley, the Astronomer Royal after whom Halley's Comet is named. Like the rest of Oxford, the college suffered an academic decline in the 18th century: according to the philosopher Jeremy Bentham, who became an undergraduate there in 1760 at the age of 12, the members of Queen's in his time 'were all either stupid or dissipated. I learnt nothing. I played at tennis once or twice . . .' During the 19th-century period of revival the art critic Walter Pater was an undergraduate at Queen's. The 20th century brought the first notable additions to the buildings for 200 years. There could hardly be a greater contrast than that between the discreet Queen's Lane Quad (next to St Edmund Hall), designed by Marshall Sisson – incorporating old houses and shops on the High Street – and Sir James Stirling's Florey Building (1968-70), which is anything but discreet. It is named after Lord Florey, provost of Queen's, who developed the curative properties of penicillin.

St Edmund Hall

St Edmund Hall, familiarly known as Teddy Hall, became a college as recently as 1957. Before then it was the last surviving medieval hall in Oxford (see p. 6). First recorded in 1317, its name derives from the tradition that St Edmund of Abingdon gave lectures in a house on its site when he taught theology at the University in the early 13th century. Being a hall rather than a college it had no individual founder, but was set up by a group of graduates who maintained the buildings as a boarding-house for undergraduates. It had no endowments and was financed entirely by undergraduates' fees; its principals often contributed

59 *St Edmund Hall: left, the Front Quad's 16th-century north range, the oldest part of the college; right, the chapel (1680); in the foreground, the well-head*

to building expenses out of their own pockets. For centuries St Edmund Hall had close links with nearby Queen's College (as St Mary's Hall had with Oriel College); in 1559 the University granted Queen's the privilege of electing the hall's principals. However, St Edmund Hall retained an independent character, and finally severed all formal links with Queen's in 1934.

The tiny Front Quad of St Edmund Hall is for many people their favourite place in Oxford (**59**). Nothing in the mundane 17th-century front on Queen's Lane leads the visitor to expect the intimate charm of the quad beyond. The earliest part is the eastern section of the north range (1596), extended and faithfully copied to the west in 1741. To the east is the classical front of the chapel (1680), which contains stained glass by Burne-Jones and William Morris (1865) – their earliest work in Oxford – and an altar-piece by Ceri Richards (1957-8). The well in front of the chapel, which supplied the hall with drinking water in the Middle Ages, was reopened in 1927, when the present well-head was erected.

To the north of Front Quad is the Church of St Peter-in-the-East (now the college's library) and its graveyard, a perfect setting for open-air study in the summer (**60**). The buildings of Upper Quad (1968-70) were designed by Kenneth Stevens and include a new dining hall. Although the plan is ingenious, the effect of squeezing these relatively massive buildings into such a confined space is rather vertiginous, like an elephant balancing on one leg.

St John's College

St John's College was founded in 1557 by Sir Thomas White, a leading member of the Merchant Taylors' Company and one-time Lord Mayor of London. His

▲**60** *St Peter-in-the-East, now the library of St Edmund Hall; there has been a church on this site since Anglo-Saxon times. The nave and chancel are Norman, as is the slightly earlier crypt*

►**61** *St John's College: the west doorway and arcades of Canterbury Quadrangle (1631-6); the statue of Queen Henrietta Maria, wife of Charles I, is by Charles' sculptor, Le Sueur, who probably also made the statue of the Earl of Pembroke in the Schools Quadrangle (**16**)*

new college, named after John the Baptist, the patron saint of tailors, was intended to train orthodox clergymen to combat Protestant heresy. The site and original buildings belonged to St Bernard's College, established in 1437 by Archbishop Chichele, founder of All Souls, for student monks of the Cistercian order. St Bernard's was dissolved in 1540, sold to Christ Church and then bought by White, who was guided by a dream in which he saw its buildings, surrounded by elms.

St Bernard's had been built very slowly and was still incomplete when White acquired it: he roofed the east range and converted the kitchen into a hall. Throughout the 16th century St John's was known to harbour Catholic sympathisers, including amongst its fellows Edmund Campion (martyred 1581). In the 17th century its High Church and Royalist reputation was enhanced by the presidency of William Laud (1611-21), archbishop of Canterbury and a loyal supporter of Charles I. He financed Canterbury Quadrangle (1631-6; **61**). The designer of these arcaded and richly decorated buildings is unknown, although Nicholas Stone, architect of the Botanic Garden gates and St Mary's south porch, is an attractive suggestion. The quad was opened in 1636 with a feast and a play for Charles I and Queen Henrietta Maria, whose statues surmount the west and east entrances. The south range incorporates an earlier building, the library (1596-1601), which Laud had extended into the east range. Laud was executed in 1645, having been convicted of high treason at the instigation of Parliament. His body was interred in the chapel in 1663, and his ghost is said to walk in the library.

The hall was remodelled in the 18th century: the stone screen (1742) was designed by James Gibbs. The chapel was given its present appearance in 1843; the gilded and garlanded eagle lectern (1773) should not be overlooked. The beautiful gardens, which George III thought the finest in his dominions, were first landscaped in 1748.

St John's possesses some of the best 20th-century architecture in Oxford. In North Quad are the famous 'beehives' (1958-60), polygonal undergraduate accommodation designed by the Architects Co-Partnership (**62**), and between the garden and St Giles is the Sir Thomas White Building (1975), an elegant masterpiece by Arup Associates (**63**).

Trinity College

In 1286 land between Broad Street and Parks Road was granted to the monks of Durham Abbey, who founded a college there for theological students. The abbey was dissolved in 1540 and Durham College passed to Osney Abbey (later Oxford Cathedral). It was purchased in 1555 by Sir Thomas Pope, a wealthy civil servant, who founded Trinity College in its place.

The buildings stand well back from Broad Street behind a leafy garden; originally they were approached by a narrow walled lane. Durham Quad is on the site of Durham College. The east range (1417-21), which contains the library, is the only surviving part of the old college. In 1618 the monks' hall collapsed, and a new one was erected in its place on the west side of the quad, in very conventional Jacobean Gothic style. The interior was remodelled, to rather boring effect, in 1774. The north range of the quad dates from 1728; the south range contains the gate-tower and the chapel (1691-4; **64**), one of Oxford's greatest architectural glories. The designer is unknown; Wren was consulted, but did not draw up the plans. The finely proportioned exterior carries on its parapet statues of Geometry, Astronomy, Theology and Medicine, as well as urns spouting copper flames. The interior is unforgettable. The beautiful panelling is in juniper and walnut; the limewood carving on the reredos, of cherubs' heads poking through foliage and fruit, is so outstandingly fine that Grinling Gibbons seems the only possible author, although there is no documentary evidence of his working here. The lavishly decorated stucco ceiling incorporates paintings by Pierre Berchet. A glass-fronted cupboard to the left of the altar contains the founder's monument (*c*1567), erected by his widow; Pope and his two wives are buried beneath.

In 1668 Wren designed a new building, which initially stood alone but now forms the north range of the three-sided Garden Quad. His work was largely obscured in the 19th century by the addition of a third storey. Garden Quad faces onto a long lawn, at the end of which is a wrought-iron gate erected in 1713. According to tradition, this will be opened only when a Jacobite king returns to the throne of England – but the 'gate' is in fact a grille, and cannot be opened. In the 19th century Sir Thomas Jackson designed new buildings for Front Quad in his usual quasi-Jacobean style. Behind them is the modern Cumberbatch Quad (1964-8), incorporating the huge underground bookroom of Blackwell's bookshop.

Famous men educated at Trinity include Cardinal Newman, leader of the

► **65** *University College: a view into the Master's Garden, with the gables of Radcliffe Quad (1716-19) behind*

▼ **64** *Trinity College: the 17th-century gate-tower and chapel*

Oxford Movement (see p. 13) until his conversion to Roman Catholicism (there is a bust of him at the east end of Wren's range of Garden Quad). The writer John Aubrey studied here in the 1640s, and several of his anecdotes concern Oxford life of that period. Sir Richard Burton, the explorer and translator of *The Arabian Nights*, entered Trinity in 1840, but disliked Oxford so much that he had himself sent down for illegally driving a dog-cart: he told his family that he had been awarded a long holiday for getting a particularly brilliant degree, joined the army and left the country.

► **66** *Wadham College: the centre-piece of Front Quad (1610-13) bears statues of the founder and his wife, Nicholas and Dorothy Wadham, a statue of James I above and the royal coat of arms at the top*

University College

Until the 19th century University College (familiarly 'Univ.') officially regarded King Alfred as its founder; in 1874 it had a feast to celebrate its thousandth anniversary. This legend was largely the fabrication of medieval lawyers. In 1380 the college became involved in a long legal battle over some land. By claiming King Alfred as its founder, it was able to call itself royal property and have the dispute moved to the King's Court for a speedy (and favourable) decision. A statue of King Alfred, formerly over the main entrance, has been replaced by one of Queen Anne, but his portrait is set into the chimney-piece in the hall.

In fact the college dates from 1249, when William of Durham, a scholar and ecclesiastic, bequeathed 310 marks to the University for the maintenance of at least ten poor theological students. The University bought the necessary land but apparently took no further action till 1280, when at the prompting of William's executors plans were drawn up for the foundation of a college. At first this was very small, consisting of only four MAs, and limited to men from Durham.

Nothing remains of the medieval structure, for the whole college was rebuilt in the 17th century. Front Quad was begun in 1633; completion (*c*1677) was delayed by the Civil War. Its plan and Gothic style were closely modelled on the quads at Oriel and Wadham; the prettily shaped gables (**65**) are identical to those in Jesus College Inner Quad. The hall, drastically remodelled in the 18th century, was returned to something like its original state in 1904. The hammer-beam roof is original – the date 1656 is carved on it. The chapel was altered in 1862 by Scott, who installed the present roof. The opulent stained glass (1641) was designed by Abraham van Linge; most of the 17th-century woodwork survives, including the beautiful screen (1694). There are several monuments by John Flaxman, most strikingly the large tablet (1794) commemorating the orientalist Sir William Jones, the first man in England to master Sanskrit and a judge of the High Court of Calcutta. He is depicted writing his massive digest of the Hindu law of India, watched admiringly by several natives.

Over the inner arch of the entrance tower is a statue of James II, erected in 1687 – apart from the bronze statue by Grinling Gibbons in Trafalgar Square the only existing statue of this unpopular king. Its presence here is due to the election as master in 1676 of Obadiah Walker, a discreet Roman Catholic who supported James' religious views. When James became king Mass was celebrated in the Master's Lodge and the townspeople reacted angrily, but within the college there was tolerance – in sharp contrast to the bitter struggle at Magdalen. However, Walker was ejected when James fled the country.

Dr John Radcliffe, who financed the Radcliffe Camera, bequeathed money to

University College for a new quadrangle (1716-19). Its faithful imitation of the Gothic of Front Quad is remarkably conservative, and contrasts with the contemporary classical buildings of the Queen's College across the High Street. There is a statue of Radcliffe over the entrance, facing the quad.

University College's most famous undergraduate was Shelley; he was expelled in 1811 for publishing a pamphlet entitled *The Necessity of Atheism* and circulating it amongst the heads of the colleges and several bishops. In 1894 the college was given Edward Onslow Ford's memorial to the poet, which had been intended for his grave in the Protestant Cemetery at Rome but was rejected as too large. It was installed in a domed chamber in the north-west corner of Front Quad. The life-size figure represents Shelley's drowned body as it was found in 1822 on the shore near Viareggio. For years a source of embarrassment and subject of mockery, Ford's disturbingly sensuous masterpiece has at last come to be appreciated.

► **67** *Wadham College Chapel: the east window (1622) is the work of Bernard van Linge, who with his brother, Abraham, designed much of Oxford's 17th-century stained glass (see especially Lincoln and University Colleges). The stalls and panelling below the window are 19th century. The lectern is dated 1691*

Wadham College

Nicholas Wadham of Merifield in Somerset was on very bad terms with most of his relatives, so he decided to devote the bulk of his fortune to the founding of a new college in Oxford. After his death in 1609 his energetic widow Dorothy completed his plans. She purchased land (the site of an Augustinian friary) and supervised every detail of the building of Front Quad (1610-13). The designer and master mason was William Arnold, from Somerset (he also worked on Montacute House) – a reflection of the college's strong links with the west country.

Front Quad has survived substantially unaltered. It is obsessively symmetrical: for example, the entrance to the chapel on the left side of the east range is matched by a false door on the right. A centre-piece between the doors (**66**) resembles the contemporary one in Merton College Fellows' Quad. The chapel (**67**), in the traditional Oxford T-shape, contains much fine 17th-century woodwork, especially the beautiful screen (1613). The hall has an ornate screen (1612) and its original hammer-beam roof. Wadham was noted for intellectual distinction during the wardenship of John Wilkins (1648-59), a founder of the Royal Society, whose original members, including Christopher Wren, first met at the college. The brilliant and dissolute poet John Wilmot, earl of Rochester, was admitted in 1660.

The west range of Back Quad contains the sole addition to the original buildings before the 20th century, a three-storey house of 1693-4. The east range is a drab structure of 1951-4. To the south is a superbly successful blend of old houses and shops on Holywell Street and new buildings by Gillespie, Kidd and Coia (1971-2). The shady and secluded gardens were landscaped in 1796. Behind the chapel is a frighteningly legless statue of the classicist C. M. Bowra (warden 1939-70). Part of the garden wall beyond has been incorporated into Wadham's Ashraf Pahlavi Library (completed 1977). This was designed by the architects of the Holywell buildings and financed by the Iranian Imperial Foundation; it is named after the sister of the late Shah. The building also contains undergraduate accommodation and a new Junior Common Room.

Wadham owns the Holywell Music Room, the oldest public room in England specifically designed for music. It was erected 1742-8 by a University Music Club, and is now used by the Music Faculty for regular concerts.

Worcester College

Like Trinity and St John's, Worcester College has its origins in a monastic educational establishment dissolved by Henry VIII. In 1283 Sir John Giffard, as an act of penance, granted some of the land on which the college now stands to Gloucester Abbey, which founded Gloucester College there. In 1298 the land was regranted to the Benedictine order as a whole. Many abbeys maintained separate quarters in the college and subscribed to the erection of a hall, chapel and library for their common use. Of these public buildings nothing survives, but six 15th-century sets of chambers remain and now form the south side of the main quadrangle, looking like a picturesque row of cottages (**68**). Each was maintained by a different abbey: the coats of arms of the abbeys of Glastonbury, Malmesbury, Canterbury and Pershore decorate four of the doorways (possibly not the ones to which they originally belonged).

Gloucester College was dissolved in 1541. For a time it seemed that the buildings might become the bishop of Oxford's palace. The chapel and hall were demolished and the rest decayed; when St John's College bought the buildings in 1560 they were inhabited only by 'two old priests'. St John's repaired and maintained the old college as an academic hall, with a fellow of St John's as principal. In the 17th century Gloucester Hall educated the poet Richard Lovelace and Kenelm Digby, the writer and diplomat. After the Civil War its fortunes declined. In 1693 the principal, Benjamin Woodroffe, decided to turn it into a seminary for theological students of the Greek Church, who would be sent from Syria and Greece at the expense of the Levant Company. This scheme only worked for nine years. Woodroffe then heard that Sir Thomas Cookes of Bentley, Worcestershire, was planning to give Oxford £10,000 towards the foundation of a new college or the extension of an existing one.

68, 69 Worcester College: (above) *the 15th-century south range, which was originally part of the monastic Gloucester College, contrasts with* (right) *the 18th-century north range of the quad*

82

Having rapidly drawn up statutes for 'Worcester College', Woodroffe urged that Gloucester Hall was suitable for transformation into a college. Cookes died without specifying where his money was to go; Woodroffe went bankrupt, was imprisoned for debt and died. Magdalen Hall (see Hertford College) was a favourite candidate for the benefaction, but in 1713 Cookes' trustees decided to give the money to Gloucester Hall, and Worcester College was founded a year later.

Further endowments in 1717 enabled the new college to erect its own buildings. The architect, Dr George Clarke of All Souls, took advice from his friend Hawksmoor, though the designs were not strictly followed in the execution. It was intended to demolish all the medieval fabric, but money ran out after the erection of the austere east range facing Beaumont Street – incorporating the hall, chapel and library – and the north range (1753-9; **69**). At the north-west corner of the quad is the Provost's Lodging (1773-6), an elegant Palladian villa designed by Henry Keene. The delightful contrast between the medieval and classical buildings is enhanced by the view of the college's famous gardens through the open side of the quad.

Nothing more was built at Worcester until the 20th century. The interiors of the hall and chapel were designed by James Wyatt but redecorated by William Burges in 1864. The hall has since been restored according to Wyatt's original design, but the chapel remains as vulgarly opulent as Burges left it, a dimly lit and thoroughly enjoyable mixture of Renaissance and early Christian styles. The stained glass was designed by Henry Holiday, the first illustrator of Lewis Carroll's *The Hunting of the Snark*.

In 1744-5 the college acquired extensive meadows to the north and west from St John's; they were landscaped in 1817, when the tranquil and half-hidden lake was made, and form a romantic setting for the summer play by the college dramatic society, the Buskins, and the antics of Worcester's ornamental ducks.

19th- and 20th-century colleges

Keble College, opened in 1870, was the first new college in Oxford for over a century. It is named after the Rev. John Keble, a religious poet and one of the founders of the Oxford Movement (see p. 13). It was intended to strengthen Oxford's traditional links with the Church of England and to help make a university education available to men of limited means. The architect was William Butterfield, who also designed Balliol chapel. Keble is not beautiful, and was not intended to be; it is earnest, harsh and overwhelming (what the Victorians called 'real'). Butterfield was allowed to exercise his passion for polychromatic brickwork on a massive scale; the result suggests a crouching dinosaur in a Fair Isle sweater. The huge chapel (**70**) towers above Liddon Quad. Its interior is lavishly decorated with mosaics. In a side chapel to the south is Holman Hunt's painting *The Light of the World*, given to the college in 1873. To supplement its meagre funds Keble charged visitors who wished to look at the famous picture; Holman Hunt was so enraged that he painted a replica, which hangs in St Paul's Cathedral. A novel feature of the college's design is the arrangement of rooms along corridors, whereas in the older colleges access to rooms is by staircase. Keble's tradition of architectural ugliness has been continued with a new building by Ahrends, Burton and Koralek (1973-7). The side that faces the college is a coil of tinted glass; on the outside is a fortress-like brick wall which arrogantly overshadows pretty little Blackhall Road.

Before state grants became widely available the University was greatly

▼ **70** *Keble College: Liddon Quad is dominated by the college's huge chapel (1868-82). Ruskin gave up his daily walks in the Parks to avoid having to look at it*

concerned to find ways to enable poor men to study at Oxford. In 1868 its statutes were changed to allow students to be members without being attached to a college, so that they could avoid the expense of college life. They were supervised by Delegates based in the Clarendon Building, but no central meeting-place was provided, so the students themselves hired rooms in Broad Street, on a site known as St Catherine's Chapel. In 1883, in recognition of this self-created corporate spirit, the University erected a building for the students' use next to the Examination Schools in the High Street. In 1934 'St Catherine's Society' moved to new buildings in St Aldate's, south of Christ Church (now inhabited by the Music Faculty). With the introduction of state grants the society lost its main purpose, and in 1963 it became an ordinary undergraduate college. As **St Catherine's College** it moved into new buildings (1964) by the Danish architect Arne Jacobsen, who designed everything, including the furniture and cutlery – even the bricks were specially made. In the formality of its layout and its pure proportions St Catherine's possesses great beauty (**71**); the extensive planting of creepers and shrubs has softened its aloof appearance.

St Peter's College, like St Catherine's, was originally intended for poor students alone. Dr F. J. Chavasse retired as bishop of Liverpool in 1923 and came to live in Oxford, where he had been rector of St Peter-le-Bailey. He found his old church (an early work of Basil Champneys) dilapidated and its congregation almost gone, so he decided to convert the church and its adjacent property into a hall for the accommodation of undergraduates of limited means (especially candidates for holy orders). St Peter's Hall became a full college in 1961; the old church is now its chapel. The college incorporates some of the buildings of New Inn Hall, one of the old academic halls (see p. 6), founded as Trilleck's Inn in the 14th century. They include the dining hall (1832 and subsequently remodelled), named after James Hannington, the first bishop of Eastern Equatorial Africa, who was killed by savages in 1855. The Master's Lodgings (1827-9) were formerly the offices of the Oxford Canal Company.

Ruskin College was founded in 1899 by Mr and Mrs Vrooman to make the privileges of an Oxford education available to working men and women, a purpose which it has uninterruptedly preserved. It moved to its present buildings in Walton Street in 1913. Ruskin College is not part of the University; it is financed and governed by trade unions and other workers' organisations.

The numerous theological colleges established in Oxford in the latter part of the 19th century are also not colleges of the University; they are 'permanent private halls' whose members may study for University examinations, usually as part of their training for holy orders. The Society of Jesus established **Campion Hall** in 1896 in buildings in Brewer Street designed by Lutyens. **St Benet's Hall** was founded in 1897 for monks from Ampleforth; it was followed in 1910 by **Greyfriars** in the Iffley Road for members of the Franciscan order and in 1921 by **Blackfriars** in St Giles for the Dominicans. **Pusey House**, named after one of the leaders of the Oxford Movement, was built in 1884 as a theological college which would maintain Pusey's High Church ideals. In 1979 it was decided to incorporate it into St Cross College (see p. 90). In 1889 **Mansfield College** was opened, to train men for the Congregational ministry. It is now no longer an exclusively theological college and accepts students to read most subjects. Its original buildings were designed by Basil Champneys. Next door is **Manchester College**, for Unitarians, founded in Manchester in 1786 and moved to Oxford in 1888. The chapel contains a superb series of

▲ **72** *St Cross Churchyard. The church dates from the 12th century and is now used by St Catherine's as its chapel*

stained glass windows by Burne-Jones. **Wycliffe Hall**, an evangelical Church of England college, was established in 1877. **Regent's Park College**, founded in 1810 in London to train Baptist ministers, moved to Oxford in 1940.

It took many years for women to be accepted as full members of the University, although they had been associated with Oxford for centuries in the founding and endowment of men's colleges. In 1878 Dr Talbot of Keble, who had been impressed by a visit to Girton College, Cambridge, proposed with several other dons the creation of a small hall to be run on Church of England principles for women 'desirous of availing themselves of the special privileges which Oxford offers of higher education'. The religious nature of this proposed foundation aroused criticism, so it was decided to establish two halls, one (Lady Margaret Hall) to be Church of England and the other (Somerville) to be undenominational. Nevertheless, there was still fierce opposition to the whole idea of women's colleges, one eminent don claiming that it 'runs counter to the wisdom and experience of all the centuries of Christendom'. **Lady Margaret Hall** was named in honour of Lady Margaret Beaufort (Henry VII's mother) at the suggestion of the first principal, Elizabeth Wordsworth, because 'she was a gentlewoman, a scholar, and a saint, and after having been three times married she took a vow of celibacy. What more could be expected of any woman?' The college initially occupied a house in Norham Gardens, and later expanded in its spacious grounds; the massive, mostly neo-Georgian, buildings include a Byzantine chapel (1931) by Sir Giles Gilbert Scott and two residential towers (1972) by M. Christophe Gillet. **Somerville College** was named after Mary

◄ **71** *St Catherine's College (1960-4), designed by Arne Jacobsen: the Bernard Sunley lecture rooms*

◄ **73** *Lady Margaret Hall: looking towards the gardens which run down to the Cherwell*

Somerville, a distinguished early Victorian astronomer. From its original premises in Walton Manor it has developed the surrounding cramped site between Little Clarendon Street and the Radcliffe Infirmary.

Not all female students were accommodated in these two colleges: some preferred to study at home. Their interests were looked after by a special committee for 'home students'. Gradually they established a corporate spirit and hired rooms for their common use in the High Street in 1898. In 1929 a trust was set up to erect a building for them between the Banbury and Woodstock Roads, designed by Scott. In 1942 the Society of Home Students became St Anne's Society and in 1952 **St Anne's College**. Its more recent buildings include a dining hall by Gerald Banks (1958-60) looking onto the garden, with a lurid mural by Stefan Kapp on the outside wall, and residential buildings and the Founder's Tower – the college's entrance gate – by Howell, Killick, Partridge and Amis (1966).

By 1894 all University examinations had been opened to women – a remarkably rapid progress in view of the earlier opposition to women's colleges. In the interim **St Hugh's College** had been established (1886) in a house on Norham Road by Elizabeth Wordsworth, who named it after the 12th-century bishop of Lincoln and in honour of her father, also bishop of Lincoln. Its first principal was the formidable Miss Moberly (who once met the ghost of Marie Antoinette at Versailles). Dorothea Beale, principal of Cheltenham Ladies' College, bought land in Oxford for a new college in the same year, but it was not until 1893 that she settled on the lovely 18th-century Cowley House, by the river near Magdalen Bridge, as the nucleus of **St Hilda's College**. Both St Hugh's and St Hilda's have striking (and very different) examples of modern architecture – the Wolfson Building of St Hugh's (1964-6) by David Roberts, in cheerful red brick, and St Hilda's Garden Building (1968-70) by Alison and Peter Smithson, a simple square structure laced up in timber braces.

In 1894 the University began to consider giving degrees to women (17 years after London University had created its first female graduates). Fierce controversy in the following two years ended in Congregation's rejecting the proposal to admit women to BA degrees. The question was reopened in 1907 by the University's new Chancellor, Lord Curzon, who argued that since Oxford was providing women with a university education, it was foolish to 'yield the reality while withholding the name'; but his advice was not taken until 1920, and women's colleges did not achieve full collegiate status until 1959. For years Oxford had far fewer undergraduate places for women than for men; since 1974 this imbalance has been rectified as more and more colleges have become co-residential. In 1981 only four single-sex colleges remained: one for men (Oriel) and three for women (St Hilda's, St Hugh's and Somerville).

In 1937 Viscount Nuffield, the founder of Oxford's motor industry, gave the University land to the north of the Castle mound and £900,000 for the building and endowment of **Nuffield College** as 'a centre of research, especially by cooperation between academic and non-academic people', primarily in the field of social sciences. The foundation stone of this graduate college was laid in 1949. The buildings, in a domestic neo-Cotswold style, are generally despised for their total lack of aesthetic interest, but Lord Nuffield wanted a building that looked like an old college (he rejected some neo-Byzantine designs as too outlandish), and the finished structure, however dull, does successfully convey the traditional tranquillity of college life. The tower, topped by a little spire, is

the library bookstack. The chapel, a tiny room tucked away at the top of a staircase, has dazzling stained glass by John Piper.

The need for more graduate colleges became urgent after World War II, when the number of graduates rapidly increased, and four were founded in the next 20 years. **St Antony's College** (1948) was founded by M. Antonin Besse, a wealthy French merchant who had been impressed by the quality of Oxford graduates he employed. It moved in 1950 into the premises of the Society of the Holy Trinity (built 1866-8). Nearby is a new block, which contains the college's dining hall, designed by Howell, Killick, Partridge and Amis (1968-70). St Antony's students study history, politics and economics. **Linacre College** (1962) was established in buildings to the south of Christ Church vacated by St Catherine's, and became a full college in 1965. Thomas Linacre was a fellow of All Souls, who in 1518 founded the Royal College of Physicians. The college subsequently moved to Cherwell Edge, a house on the corner of St Cross and South Parks Roads, and its surrounding buildings. **St Cross College**, founded in 1965, occupies the buildings of Pusey House. **Wolfson College**, originally called Iffley College, was renamed after it received a huge endowment from the Wolfson Foundation. Its buildings, by Powell and Moya, have been much admired. The drab materials (off-white concrete and grey pebble-dash) and the large scale of the design could have been depressing, but the ingenious layout and the idyllic setting, in meadows beside the Cherwell, give the visitor constantly varying and beautiful views (**74**). In 1979 **Green College** was opened to the north of the Radcliffe Infirmary. It incorporates the former University Observatory (**75**), part of which is used as the dining hall. This college is entirely devoted to the postgraduate study of medicine and was named after its benefactors, Dr and Mrs Cecil Green of Dallas, Texas.

▲**74** *Wolfson College, a graduate college designed by Powell and Moya. The River Cherwell is spanned by an elegant footbridge; in the foreground is a harbour for punts*

►**75** *Green College: the old University Observatory (1772-94), begun by Keene and completed by Wyatt, and now converted into a dining hall and common rooms. The reliefs of the winds on each of the eight sides and the lead group of Hercules and Atlas supporting a globe are by Bacon. Below the tower are reliefs of signs of the zodiac*

4 Life in the Modern University

The daily workings of the University occasionally manifest themselves in a picturesque ceremony, but mostly they are hidden from visitors' eyes. The titular head of the University is the Chancellor, usually an eminent statesman or member of the royal family – Harold Macmillan (Prime Minister 1957-63) was elected Chancellor in 1960. He visits the University regularly and every June presides over the ceremony known as the Encaenia, at which he confers honorary degrees on distinguished people whom the University has decided to honour (**78**).

Actual authority is exercised by the Vice-Chancellor, who is elected every four years. He or she may in theory be any MA (Master of Arts) resident in Oxford, but is usually the head of one of the colleges. The Vice-Chancellor has a cabinet called the Hebdomadal Council (so named because it meets once a week). The 18 members of the Council are elected by the entire body of MAs resident in Oxford, known collectively as Congregation. Congregation has the right to vote on any decree of the Council which six of its members oppose; such a democratic university constitution is paralleled in Britain only in Cambridge. According to its statutes Oxford is ultimately governed by Convocation, which includes every Oxford MA in the world, but in practice Convocation is not called upon to make any decisions apart from electing the Professor of Poetry (once every five years) and the Chancellor: real power is vested in Congregation alone.

Subordinate to the Vice-Chancellor and the Council are the Registrar (the University's chief secretary) and the Secretary to the Curators of the Chest, who is responsible for financial matters. Both these officials have charge of large departments housed in the University offices on Little Clarendon Street. The Council has little direct say in academic matters, for traditionally the organisation of teaching and the curriculum is a matter for the colleges and the faculties. The central body controlling the finances of teaching and research is the General Board of the Faculties. Within the University there are also large semi-autonomous institutions, such as the Bodleian Library and the Ashmolean Museum, which are run by committees composed largely of dons and known as the Delegates of the particular organisation.

Other important officials are the Proctors, two dons appointed annually to perform a wide range of functions mostly related to the undergraduates (students who have not taken their first degree), such as licensing undergraduate motor cars and supervising the finances of many University clubs and societies. Traditionally the Proctors represent the authority of the Vice-

◄ **76** *New College dining hall. The founder's portrait hangs in the centre of the wall behind high table, surrounded by portraits of eminent members of the college*

Chancellor; they are seen at many University functions, carrying a chained copy of the Statutes that they enforce and attended by the University's police force, the four bowler-hatted 'Bulldogs'. The once-familiar sight of a bulldog in pursuit of an errant undergraduate is depicted on the sign of the Bulldog public house, in St Aldate's.

The relationship between the University and the colleges is vague and informal. The colleges are self-governing institutions, in no way administered by the University. Each college (like the University) has its own statutes, which can only be altered with the consent of the Queen in Council. Although the colleges are in effect subordinate to the University, which is the degree-giving body, their formal obligations to it do not go much beyond setting aside a proportion of their fellowships for professors and paying an annual tax, whereby the richer colleges subsidise the poorer (the difference in wealth between the rich colleges, such as Magdalen and Christ Church, and the poorest – all the womens' colleges – is vast). The University receives its income directly from the Government; the colleges live off their endowments and the fees they charge their members. In practice the most important link between the two is that the majority of the University's teaching staff hold college fellowships.

Each college has a head, in some colleges called the master and in others the warden, provost, president, rector or principal. He or she is elected by the fellows (except at Christ Church, where the dean is appointed by the Crown). The master is usually a distinguished academic, or perhaps a politician retired from public life. Other important college figures are the vice-master and the bursar (who supervises the college's finances). Most colleges have a chaplain,

▼77 *New College Chapel: the altar, and the stone statues of the reredos which were installed in the 19th century to replace those smashed by 16th-century reformers. Although attendance is no longer compulsory, chapel and the music associated with it remain an important part of collegiate life*

78 The annual ceremony of the Encaenia: the University's Chancellor, Harold Macmillan, processes to the Sheldonian Theatre, where he will confer honorary degrees. He is preceded by the Bedels carrying their 16th-century maces. The procession is about to enter the Schools Quadrangle through the main gateway, which is opened only on ceremonial occasions

although attendance at chapel is no longer compulsory for undergraduates, as it still was at the beginning of this century. The college is governed jointly by the master and fellows, the senior members of the college elected on the basis of their academic achievements. Although much of their time is devoted to teaching, for many of the fellows their own research is equally or more important. The teaching of every subject studied in the University is organised by a faculty, composed of committees of dons (sometimes with undergraduate representation) responsible for arranging lectures and seminars as well as organising the curriculum and setting examinations. The faculties at Oxford are far less important than at most other universities, since they have almost no responsibility for individual tuition, which is the preserve of the colleges.

Undergraduates are selected by the college to which they apply and not by the University, which merely determines the basic academic requirements which all undergraduate applicants must meet before they can matriculate (become members of the University). The applicant's choice of college is usually influenced by school or family connections, or by factors such as size (in 1980 St Anne's had 389 undergraduates and Christ Church 386, whereas Corpus Christi had 187 and Merton 227). The traditional character of the college – Christ Church aristocratic, Balliol studious and liberal, Jesus Welsh and St Edmund Hall hearty – may also be influential, as it certainly was in the past, but these reputations are gradually being diluted. Most colleges are now co-residential: in 1981 only four colleges remained single-sex.

Successful application depends on the candidate's performance at A-level (final school examinations taken at 18), in the Colleges' Joint Examination taken in the November preceding entry and in interviews with one or two dons at the candidate's first choice of college. Increasing numbers of entrants apply before taking A-levels and may be offered places conditional on their results. Entrance scholarships and exhibitions, awarded on the basis of performance in the Colleges' Examination, are more important for the prestige than for the money they bring (usually £60 a year for a scholarship and £40 for an exhibition). Scholarships may also be awarded as a reward for getting a first (being placed in the first class) in a University examination. The colleges are fiercely competitive academically; the Norrington Table, published every year, gives each college points on the basis of its examination results, and to come top is regarded as a great achievement.

The usual undergraduate course is three years, except for Classics – known as Greats – which lasts four. Each year is divided into three terms of eight weeks each, called Michaelmas, Hilary and Trinity. Almost every undergraduate spends at least one and usually two years living in college; for the rest of the time he or she lives 'out', either in college-owned hostels or lodgings or in a shared house somewhere in Oxford's suburbs. Accommodation in college can range from grand but spartan sets of rooms in ancient college buildings to small comfortable modern bedsitters. The college provides meals throughout the term, traditionally of deplorable quality (in contrast to the frequently superb food and wine enjoyed by the fellows). Dinner in some of the older colleges can be very formal; it is one of the few remaining occasions when the undergraduates must wear gowns, and there is often a lengthy Latin grace and an impressive display of college silver. The master and fellows usually sit at high table on a dais at one end of the hall, with the undergraduates on benches at long tables below (**76**). Some colleges preserve ancient traditions at dinner time. At the Queen's College, dinner is announced by a trumpet. Sconcing, though frowned on by college authorities, still goes on: this is a penalty for infringing

▼**79** *Oxford in the summer: punts on the Cherwell*

certain arbitrary rules of conversation at dinner, for instance by mentioning academic work, or the college portraits. The offender has to drink the contents of a silver sconce cup of beer (usually about three pints) in one draught. If he succeeds – which is rare – he can return the challenge, and the bout can continue indefinitely; when it does end, the loser has to pay for all the beer that has been drunk.

The colleges are responsible for individual tuition, and every college provides teaching in almost every subject. Each undergraduate is in the care of a tutor who organises the teaching of a particular subject within the college. He or she arranges for the undergraduate to attend tutorials – hour-long, usually weekly, meetings with a don or research student who discusses the undergraduate's essay or problems set the previous week and gives work for the week to come. Some colleges also provide moral tutors, who are responsible for the under-graduates' welfare.

The timetable of any undergraduate depends very largely on his or her subject. Those studying sciences are kept busy with essential lectures and practical laboratory work, as well as tutorials, for most of the day. The arts student has more freedom to arrange his own timetable, and for him lectures are usually secondary to the all-important weekly tutorial. To qualify for a degree every undergraduate must take two University examinations, at which the wearing of subfusc (formal academic dress, including a gown) is still compulsory, and the wearing of roses in buttonholes traditional. The first examination, known as Mods (short for Moderations) in some subjects and Prelims (Preliminary examinations) in others, is usually taken during the first year. After that it may be possible to transfer to a different Honour School (as each course is known). There are no further University examinations until Finals (known as Schools), and this gives students the opportunity to enjoy themselves in their second year – many remember that summer as the most idyllic of their lives. In

addition to University examinations there are college tests known as collections, in some colleges as often as once a term. 'Collection' is also the name of the undergraduate's official termly visit to the head of his college to hear his tutor's report formally read out, and to receive words of criticism or commendation.

The period before University examinations, the fifth week of Trinity term, is known as Eights Week. For five days the college boathouses become the centre of a huge party, as crowds gather to watch the college crews race. As the river is too narrow for the boats to race abreast, they start at regular intervals and each attempts to catch and 'bump' the boats ahead (hence the races are also known as bumps). Each day the returning crews are tossed in the river, and at the end of the week, in solemn ritual, the overall winners burn their boat.

Successful candidates in the examinations of the following weeks are classed as firsts, seconds and thirds; the results are posted up inside the Examination Schools, where they are awaited by crowds of anxious undergraduates. (The High Street frontage of the Examination Schools shows a student being given a *viva voce*, a method still used to decide whether a borderline candidate should be promoted from the second class to the first.) The end of examinations is always marked by revels in the streets, as those who have finished are greeted by their friends with champagne – an activity which the Proctors try regularly to suppress, without success. The following period is full of social life, with parties throughout the day and night, concerts, plays and revues, and large formal dances in many colleges.

Those who have done well in their Schools may stay on in Oxford as research students, working in the University's libraries and laboratories for the DPhil degree (the doctorate) or for one of the other postgraduate degrees, such as BD (Bachelor of Divinity) or BCL (Bachelor of Civil Law). The graduate popu-

81 *The Union Society, the University's debating club and nursery of many of England's Prime Ministers. The earliest parts were designed by Benjamin Woodward, the architect of the University Museum; the old library contains faded frescoes and decorations by William Morris and several Pre-Raphaelite artists*

lation of Oxford has risen sharply since 1945, and now accounts for 24% of the University's student population (in 1979-80 there were 2975 graduates and 9379 undergraduates). Many research students come to Oxford having taken their first degree elsewhere: they are accommodated primarily by the graduate colleges. Some graduate students stay on in Oxford to become dons, others move away to teaching posts in other universities. Students who do not remain after taking their first degree (BA – Bachelor of Arts) can return to Oxford seven years after matriculation to take their MA degree on payment of a fee. Thereafter their formal contacts with the University are likely to be limited to attending gaudies, the college reunion dinners.

For many undergraduates social life and pastimes are as important as academic activities – and may be more important, in terms of their eventual careers. University activities attract a very high level of talent and competition; the less ambitious pursue their interest in sport, drama or music at the college level. The greatest sporting accolade is to take part in a match against Cambridge, which entitles the participant to be known as a blue and wear a dark blue blazer, if the sport is a 'major' one – such as cricket, rugby or rowing (the famous annual boat race on the Thames). Half blues are awarded if the sport is a 'minor' one, such as ice-hockey, archery or karate. Each college has its own sports ground, and there are inter-collegiate competitions in most sports. College rowing takes place on the river between Folly Bridge and Iffley Lock, a pastoral setting for chilly early-morning outings and for the summer festivities of Eights Week.

Undergraduate musical activity is centred on college orchestras and choirs and on University societies such as the Oxford University Orchestra, which mounts two or three large-scale orchestral concerts a term (often in the Sheldonian), and the Musical Club, which gives regular chamber concerts in Holywell Music Room. The largest drama society is OUDS (the Oxford University Drama Society), which stages plays in the Oxford Playhouse in Beaumont Street and provides a stepping-stone to a career in the theatre. There are also smaller, more experimental University groups. In the summer college drama societies often mount plays in college gardens.

Other societies – at any one time there are about 250 – cater for almost every conceivable interest. The best known include the Bullingdon, the resort of aristocratic huntsmen, and Vincent's, for prominent undergraduate sportsmen; the most famous is the Oxford Union Society (founded in 1825), which holds regular debates throughout the term in its buildings in St Michael's Street (**81**). The Union is traditionally a nursery for aspiring politicians – its past presidents include Gladstone, Asquith and Edward Heath. The society achieved international notoriety by its resolution in 1933 that it would 'in no circumstances fight for king and country', a result widely – but erroneously – held to be the consequence of Communist infiltration in the University and a direct cause of World War II. Those undergraduate politicians who find the Union insufficiently radical compete for office in the Students' Union, which attempts to represent students' opinions to the University.

Most of the concerts and plays staged by students are open to the public, as is choral evensong in many college chapels – notably Christ Church, Magdalen and New Colleges, which possess world-famous choirs. The varied life of the University and colleges makes a great wealth of cultural activity available to all who live in or visit Oxford.

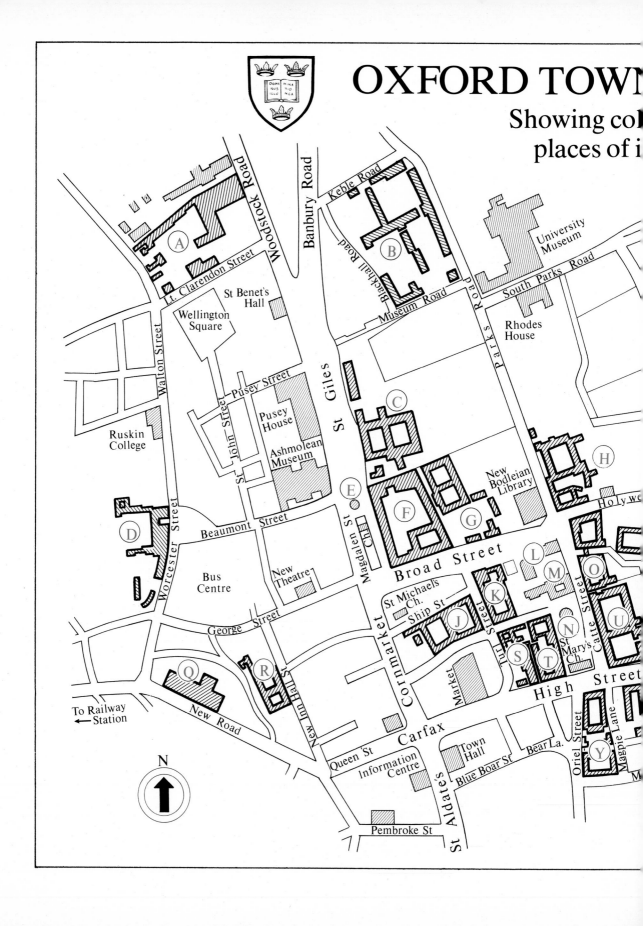

MAP (NORTH)

s and
est

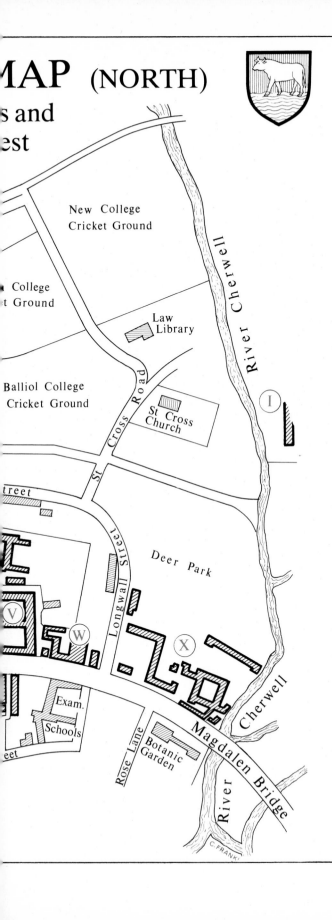

New College
Cricket Ground

College
t Ground

Balliol College
Cricket Ground

Law
Library

River Cherwell

St Cross Road

St Cross
Church

I

treet

Longwall Street

Deer Park

V

W

X

Exam.
Schools

Rose Lane

Botanic
Garden

Magdalen Bridge

River Cherwell

C. FRANK

Key

A	Somerville College
B	Keble College
C	St John's College
D	Worcester College
E	Martyrs' Memorial
F	Balliol College
G	Trinity College
H	Wadham College
I	St Catherine's College
J	Jesus College
K	Exeter College
L	Sheldonian Theatre & Clarendon Building
M	Old Bodleian Library
N	Radcliffe Camera
O	Hertford College
P	New College
Q	Nuffield College
R	St Peter's College
S	Lincoln College
T	Brasenose College
U	All Souls College
V	The Queen's College
W	St Edmund Hall
X	Magdalen College
Y	Oriel College
Z	University College

OXFORD TO

Showing colleges

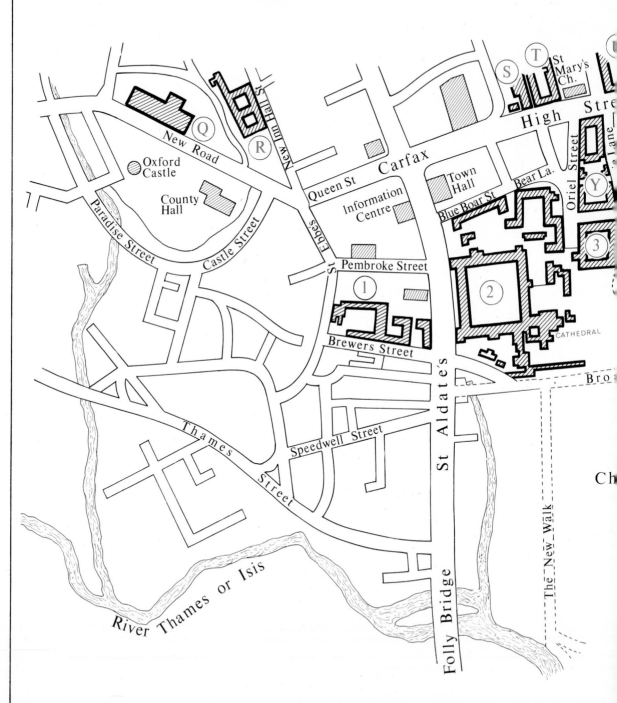